DEBUSSY

PRELUDE TO "THE AFTERNOON OF A FAUN"

An Authoritative Score

Mallarmé's Poem · Backgrounds and Sources

Criticism and Analysis

NORTON CRITICAL SCORES

BACH — **CANTATA NO. 4**
edited by Gerhard Herz

BACH — **CANTATA NO. 140**
edited by Gerhard Herz

BEETHOVEN — **SYMPHONY NO. 5 IN C MINOR**
edited by Elliot Forbes

BERLIOZ — **FANTASTIC SYMPHONY**
edited by Edward T. Cone

CHOPIN — **PRELUDES, OPUS 28**
edited by Thomas Higgins

DEBUSSY — **PRELUDE TO "THE AFTERNOON OF A FAUN"**
edited by William W. Austin

MOZART — **PIANO CONCERTO IN C MAJOR, K. 503**
edited by Joseph Kerman

MOZART — **SYMPHONY IN G MINOR, K. 550**
edited by Nathan Broder

PALESTRINA — **POPE MARCELLUS MASS**
edited by Lewis Lockwood

PURCELL — **DIDO AND AENEAS**
edited by Curtis Price

SCHUBERT — **SYMPHONY IN B MINOR ("UNFINISHED")**
edited by Martin Chusid

SCHUMANN — **DICHTERLIEBE**
edited by Arthur Komar

STRAVINSKY — **PETRUSHKA**
edited by Charles Hamm

WAGNER — **PRELUDE AND TRANSFIGURATION**
from *TRISTAN AND ISOLDE*
edited by Robert Bailey

A NORTON CRITICAL SCORE

Claude Debussy

PRELUDE TO "THE AFTERNOON OF A FAUN"

An Authoritative Score
Mallarmé's Poem · Backgrounds and Sources
Criticism and Analysis

Edited by
WILLIAM W. AUSTIN
CORNELL UNIVERSITY

W · W · NORTON & COMPANY
New York · London

Copyright © 1970 by W. W. Norton & Company, Inc.

Library of Congress Catalog Card No. 78-90991

All Rights Reserved

ISBN 393-09939-3

W. W. Norton & Company, Inc., 500 Fifth Avenue, New York, N.Y. 10110
www.wwnorton.com

W. W. Norton & Company Ltd., Castle House, 75/76 Wells Street,
London W1T 3QT

PRINTED IN THE UNITED STATES OF AMERICA

5 6 7 8 9 0

Contents

Preface vii

The History of the Poem and the Music 3

The Text of Mallarmé's Poem 21

The Score of Debussy's *Prelude* 31
    Textual Note 64

Analysis
    William W. Austin · Toward an Analytical Appreciation 71

Backgrounds and Sources
    Théodore de Banville · [Wagner, Poetry, and Music] 99
    Francis Grierson · [An American at Mallarmé's Salons, 1889–92] 101
    Stéphane Mallarmé · *From* The Evolution of Literature 107
    Mallarmé · *From* Music and Literature 112
    Mallarmé · *From* Crisis in Poetry 115
    Paul Gauguin · [Impressionism and After] 123
    Odilon Redon · [Suggestive Art] 125
    Maurice Denis · [Decadence and Neo-Traditionalism] 126
    Maurice Emmanuel · [Notes on Debussy's Conversations with Ernest Guiraud] 128

Claude Debussy · [Letters to Ernest Chausson] 132
Raymond Bonheur · [The "First Stage" of the *Faun*] 137
Gustave Doret · [The First Performance of the *Faun*] 138
Pierre Louÿs · [Letter to Debussy] 141
Grierson · [The Circle Is Now Complete] 142

Criticism and Analysis
  Alfred Bruneau · [Seeking the Exceptional] 145
  Gustave Robert · [A Style of His Own] 147
  Camille Saint-Saëns · [Letter to Maurice Emmanuel] 149
  Paul Dukas · [Reviews of Debussy's Music] 151
  Ernst Decsey · [A Jewel Among Masterpieces] 157
  Pierre Boulez · [Modern Music Begins] 160
  Jean Barraqué · [An Experiment Crowned with Success] 162

Bibliography 166

Preface

The *Prelude to "The Afternoon of a Faun"* is a classic in the repertory of orchestral music, the most famous piece by Debussy, a landmark in the general history of music, and a provocative example of the interrelations of the arts of music, poetry, and ultimately, dance. The poem by Mallarmé to which the music refers is a classic too, exerting along with all Mallarmé's work an ever-growing influence. All sorts of studies can profit from an assembly of documents and a guide through the literature.

The score itself, as published in 1894, has served for performances and studies without consideration of Debussy's own revisions. The present edition, incorporating these revisions as they are found in the copy that Debussy used when he conducted the piece in 1908–13, fulfills an important need.

For indispensable help in preparing this edition, the editor is grateful to M. Henry Goüin, who supplied a microfilm of the revised score; to Mme. Jobert-Georges, who supplied a list of discrepancies in the manuscripts held by her publishing company; to MM. André Schaeffner and François Lesure, who helped to locate these and other sources; to Mr. Edward Lockspeiser, Miss Ruth Watanabe, Professor Donald J. Grout, Professor Hans-Jost Frey, and the late Mr. Nathan Broder, for various kindnesses.

William W. Austin

The History of the Poem and the Music

The History of the Poem and the Music

In 1862, the year Claude Debussy was born, Stéphane Mallarmé was twenty, composing the first of his poems now extant, and also an essay on *L'Art pour tous* (Art for All). In this essay he envied music for the protective mystery of its notation, in contrast to the vulnerability of literature in the coming age of universal literacy. By the 1890s, when Mallarmé and Debussy were friends, the poet's envy of music had broadened and deepened; so had his musical experience; so had his poetry. By the 1960s, Mallarmé's poetry was inspiring many musicians to invent new kinds of notation, and his most famous poem, *L'Après-midi d'un faune* (The Afternoon of a Faun), claimed the interest of many more musicians and music lovers all around the world because of the Prelude that it had inspired Debussy to compose.

In 1863 Mallarmé wrote a sixteen-line poem, *Apparition*, which Debussy was to make into a song (1884). This was the only Mallarmé poem set by Debussy until 1913, when he set three more.

1863 was the year of another literary work that forms a link between Debussy and Mallarmé. The author was Théodore de Banville (1823–91), a leader of the group that called itself the Parnassians, and a pioneer in the momentous French appreciation of the work of Richard Wagner (1813–83). The young Mallarmé looked up to the Parnassians as established masters. Banville's new work was a short play, *Diane au bois* (Diana in the Wood). It was performed at the Odéon, and it was published the next year. Banville's *Diane* was among the chief sources of ideas, moods, and methods that went into Mallarmé's *Faun*.[1] For Debussy, *Diane* was to be the basis of a projected opera; he worked on it from 1882 to 1886, and then gave it up, unable to satisfy his ideal of the radically novel music for which it called.[2] Besides *Diane*, other poems of Banville inspired Debussy to write three songs and a divertissement for orchestra, *Triomphe de Bacchus* (1884). Debussy read much more of Banville's work, which helped shape his taste not only in literature but in music too. It was his carrying around a volume of Banville that first attracted his fellow student at the Conservatory, Raymond Bonheur (1851–1939), to whom he was to dedicate his Prelude to the *Faun*.[3]

In 1865 Mallarmé composed the first version of his poem, *Monologue d'un faune*. He brought it to Banville and the actor Constant Coquelin, hoping that they would arrange to perform it on the stage, perhaps at the Comédie Française. They told him it was not theatrical—it could interest no public, only fellow-poets. Accordingly, he put it in a drawer to revise it later. No one could have suspected then that after a hundred years this poem would be studied in all the stages of its refinement, interpreted and reinterpreted, praised and prized far above anything by Banville.

In 1875 a second version of the *Faun* was rejected. With the title *Improvisation du faune,* Mallarmé submitted it for publication in the Parnassians' third anthology. Now Banville, one of the three editors, thought the piece should be included "despite its lack of clarity, because of its rare musical qualities," but he was outvoted by his colleagues, François Coppée and Anatole France.

In 1876 Mallarmé published his final version, the *Églogue* printed in the present volume. It was his first book, a slim volume, elegantly bound for bibliophiles, with a line-drawing by Edouard Manet.

In 1882 the fame of the poem began to spread, with its citation in the novel *À Rebours* (Against the Grain) by J. K. Huysmans. Mallarmé

---

1. Henri Mondor, *Histoire d'un faune*, Paris, 1948, p. 86 ff. Mondor's book is the chief source of information on Mallarmé used here. Among many others, the following in English may be specially recommended: Edward Lockspeiser, *Mallarmé and Music*, in *Musical Times*, CVII (1966), 212 ff.; Joseph Chiari, *Symbolism from Poe to Mallarmé*, London, 1956; Andrew George Lehman, *The Symbolist Aesthetic in France 1885–1895*, Oxford, 1950; Robert Greer Cohn, *Toward the Poems of Mallarmé*, Berkeley, 1965.

2. Some excerpts from his 29-page manuscript may be seen in Edward Lockspeiser's book, *Debussy: His Life and Mind*, 2 vols., London, 1962–65.

3. Raymond Bonheur, *Souvenirs et impressions d'un compagnon de jeunesse*, in *Revue musicale*, VII (May 1926), 99.

wrote Huysmans a gracious letter of acknowledgment. Debussy, now twenty, probably heard of Mallarmé through Huysmans, if not a little earlier through Bonheur. It was in 1884 that he set Mallarmé's *Apparition*.

Having won various prizes at the Conservatory, Debussy took up his fellowship in Rome in 1885. That year Mallarmé began to attend the weekly Lamoureux orchestra concerts, and he published a notable essay, *Richard Wagner, rêverie d'un poète français,* in the newly founded *Revue Wagnérienne*. Mallarmé now ranked as a leading master of the most adventurous younger writers. His disciples soon included some who would in turn become leaders of the twentieth century: Paul Valéry, Paul Claudel, Marcel Proust, and André Gide; and some who were closer to Debussy: Henri de Régnier, Gabriel Mourey, André-Ferdinand Hérold, and especially Pierre Louÿs (1870–1925)—"of all my friends the one I have loved most."[4] At home on Tuesday evenings in the apartment where his daughter Geneviève served the punch, Mallarmé conducted informal seminars on poetry, developing his ideas until his death in 1898, starting them on a course that was still opening new vistas in the 1960s.[5]

Early in 1887, Debussy returned to Paris from Rome, to live again with his parents, to renew his activities as a pianist in the cabarets—especially the now famous *Chat Noir* (Black Cat)—and to try to establish himself in a career as a serious composer. Later this year, when a "definitive edition" of Mallarmé's *Églogue* was published by the *Revue indépendante,* Debussy bought at least one copy, which he gave to his friend, the young composer Paul Dukas (1865–1935). Another composer, V. E. C. Lombardi, in this same year wrote a *Glose* of the poem, a sort of Lisztian composition for piano that claimed to illustrate nearly every line of Mallarmé, quoting the appropriate words above the staff.[6] Lombardi's piece was little noticed. Whether Debussy knew it at all is a matter for conjecture. The poet René Ghil, who claimed to have developed the symbolism of Mallarmé, Verlaine, and Rimbaud into a more

---

4. Claude Debussy and Pierre Louÿs, *Correspondence,* ed. H. Borgeaud, Paris, 1945, p. 173.

5. Compare, for example, Robert Martin Adams, *Nil: Episodes in the Literary Conquest of the Void,* New York, 1966, p. 167; Hans-Jost Frey, *Mallarmé und die neue Musik,* in *Schweizerische Monatshefte,* XLVI (1966), 575; Hans Rudolf Zeller, *Mallarmé and Serial Thought,* in *Die Reihe,* VI (English edition, 1964), 5.

6. Lombardi's *Glose* is described in Suzanne Bernard, *Mallarmé et la musique,* Paris, 1959, p. 165 f., with a short musical quotation.

scientific system, "Instrumentalism," counted Lombardi as one of his disciples: Ghil wrote a review declaring that the *Glose* provided just what the poem lacked. Mallarmé and Ghil parted company about this time.

The years 1888 and 1889 were important ones in Debussy's life, marked by the first significant publications and public performances of his music, by new friendships, by new experiences of the music of Wagner and of other music, by several fascinating projects that were never completed, and by the completion of his first masterpiece, *La Damoiselle élue* (The Blessed Damozel). In both these years he made the fashionable pilgrimage to hear Wagner's works at Bayreuth. Ultimately, between 1890 and 1893, his attitude toward Wagner was fixed: no simple attitude, but a discriminating devotion to the marvels of harmony and orchestration, especially in *Parsifal,* together with a firm opposition to the overblown forms, the religious and political pretensions, and the insistent use of *leit motifs* in the *Ring*.[7] This very attitude Debussy might have adopted as early as 1885, when Saint-Saëns recommended it in his book on *Harmony and Melody* [8]; but Debussy had to decide for himself.

1889 was the year of the Paris World Exposition, where, under the shadow of the new Eiffel Tower, Debussy heard repeatedly a Javanese gamelan. Sharing with him both Bayreuth visits and exotic delights was a new friend, Robert Godet (1866–1950), an extraordinary Swiss journalist, scholar, amateur novelist, and composer.[9] Godet recalled in 1942 how, having met Debussy casually a few times, he encountered him at a concert, leaning against a wall watching an old man who was tirelessly writing in a notebook—it was Mallarmé. Godet and Debussy, with a glance, acknowledged their common impulse to peek into the notebook, and this glance, thought Godet, was more important than their previous introductions. "Indeed it was thanks to the Faun that our sympathy was born." Perhaps even then, he supposed as he reminisced, Debussy had anticipated that "he would penetrate the secrets of the poet by asking them of the Faun." [10]

---

7. Debussy, *M. Croche, anti-dilettante*, Paris, 1927, p. 143. .
8. Saint-Saëns, *Harmonie et mélodie*, Paris, 1885. See also his *Outspoken Essays on Music*, trans. F. Rothwell, London, 1922.
9. Robert Godet, *En marge de la marge*, in *Revue musicale*, VII (1926), 147; and his *Entretien préliminaire* in Debussy, *Lettres à deux amis . . . Godet et G. Jean-Aubry*, Paris, 1942. The incident described here is taken from the *Entretien*, pp. 11–13.
10. *Ibid.*, p. 13.

The History of the Poem and the Music

In January, 1889, Debussy joined the Société Nationale de Musique, a concert-giving organization founded by Saint-Saëns in 1871, which was to sponsor the *Prélude à "L'Après-midi d'un faune."* It was here that he established or deepened friendships with the composers of Bonheur's age, Vincent d'Indy (1851–1931) and Ernest Chausson (1855–99), and the publisher-patron Georges Hartmann. Also in 1889 Debussy began to know Gabrielle Dupont (1866–1945), to whom he would give the manuscript sketch of the *Faun* as a parting consolation in 1899, when he married Rosalie Texier.[11] In 1890 Debussy met the fantastic composer Erik Satie (1866–1925), to whom he was a loyal friend all his life.[12] To learn something about all these people is helpful to anyone who wishes to understand Debussy's unique personality and its development. Edward Lockspeiser's *Debussy: His Life and Mind* gives vivid accounts of many of these friends. But Lockspeiser would like to learn still more, for every bit of knowledge suggests further questions, and many of these can be answered only by guesses. Thus we may guess, despite Godet, that the idea of composing the *Faun* did not take shape before 1892; we cannot be sure.

In 1890 Debussy composed and published, in an elegant edition of 150 copies, his five songs from Baudelaire's *Fleurs du mal,* the most Wagnerian of all his music, unusually dense with chromatic complexities.[13] Another piece he withdrew from performance and publication at the very last moment, in April of the same year, at the risk of offending performers and patrons; this was his Fantasy for Piano and Orchestra, the most Franckish of all his music in form and orchestration. Perhaps the rehearsals of the Fantasy taught him lessons indispensable for his composition of the *Faun.*

In 1891 Debussy completed nothing on the scale of these works of the previous year. Evidently his thought was undergoing an obscure

---

11. This is the sketch published in facsimile by the Robert Owen Lehman Foundation, Washington, 1963. See Lockspeiser's comment on this publication, in *Music and Letters,* XLV (1964), 301.

12. For the relations between Debussy and Satie, see Austin, *Music in the 20th Century,* New York, 1966, pp. 158–163; for fresh detail in addition to this summary, see Patrick Gowers, *Satie's Rose Croix Music (1891–1895)*, in Proceedings of the Royal Musical Association, XCII (1966), 1.

13. Lawrence David Berman, *The Evolution of Tonal Thinking in the Works of Claude Debussy,* unpublished dissertation, Harvard, 1965, includes penetrating analyses of these songs, as well as the String Quartet and the Nocturnes. Though he dismisses the *Faun* abruptly, Berman's contribution is relevant to understanding its place in Debussy's whole work.

development, whose outcome in the *Faun* and other works begun in 1892 insures that historians will long continue to puzzle over it. Probably most of his energies in 1891 were devoted to an opera that he had begun in 1889 and never finished, *Rodrigue et Chimène,* on a libretto by Catulle Mendès (1841–1909). Mendès was the sort of poet Debussy's parents esteemed above the precious Banville and the incomprehensible Mallarmé, partly because he wielded some influence at the Opéra. As contributor to the *Revue Wagnérienne* and frequent pilgrim to Bayreuth, Mendès may have attracted Debussy himself before the latter's taste was perfected by association with such friends as Godet, Louÿs, and Mallarmé. At some point in 1891 the idea of *Rodrigue* became intolerable, and Debussy abandoned it.

During this period Debussy associated also with the remarkable organist-friend of Saint-Saëns, Jules de Brayer (1835?–1915?). Brayer had borrowed a copy of *Boris Godunov* that Saint-Saëns had brought back from Russia in 1876, and had proceeded to promote the study and performance of the music of Mussorgsky (1839–81). Both Debussy and Chausson borrowed *Boris* from Brayer, but just when and how much they studied it is uncertain. André Schaeffner, in a careful study of Debussy's connections with Russian music,[14] has shown that these were multiple and mingled, beginning in 1880, when he first worked for Tchaikovsky's patroness Mme. von Meck, and continuing, gradually deepening, through 1896, when Brayer's efforts culminated in a series of recitals of Mussorgsky songs. In 1891 and 1892 Brayer himself may well have been more excited about Saint-Saëns's new *Algerian Suite* for orchestra, or his *African Fantasy* for piano and orchestra, or his masterpiece, *Samson et Dalila* (this opera, though composed in 1868–74, received its first triumphant performance at the Paris Opéra in 1892).[15] The exoticism of *Samson* was novel and striking. Debussy had "deeply loved" the score as early as 1883, according to the recollections of his fellow pupil Paul Vidal.[16] There is no evidence to forbid a guess that Debussy may have been struck by the novelty, the power, and the classic balance of Saint-Saëns in 1891–92 as much as by the more radical origi-

---

14. Schaeffner, *Debussy et ses rapports avec la musique russe,* in P. Souvtchinsky, *Un Siècle de la musique russe,* Paris, 1953, I, 95. See also Schaeffner's summary essay on Debussy in Roland-Manuel, *Histoire de la musique,* Paris, 1963, II, 909; and the newly published letters from Chausson to Debussy, in *Revue de musicologie,* XLVII (1962), 49. This last modifies slightly the conclusions of Schaeffner.

15. Compare James Harding, *Saint-Saëns and His Circle,* London, 1965.

16. Paul Vidal, *Souvenirs d'Achille Debussy,* in *Revue musicale,* VII (1926), 110.

nality of Mussorgsky. The sounds of flute and harp accompanying Dalila's great aria of seduction, *Mon cœur s'ouvre à ta voix,* do anticipate some features of Debussy's *Faun*. Moreover, the main melodic refrain of this aria, "Ah! réponds à ma tendresse," with its chromatic descent and its exposed tritone, resembles the main idea of the *Faun* more closely than any particular melody of Wagner or Mussorgsky:

[Musical notation: Saint-Saëns "Ah! ré- ponds à ma ten-dres-se." and Debussy theme]

Thus it is ironic that Saint-Saëns disliked Debussy thoroughly, and condemned the *Faun* in particular as lacking any real musical idea.

In 1891 the idea of staging some version of the *Faun* was still, or again, alive for Mallarmé. A collection of his works published in Brussels, with the title *Pages,* promised a new edition of this poem for the theater. The story that Jean Dupérier, in 1957, recalled hearing from Hérold fits in here, although it omits any dates whatever and the mistake in its opening sentence arouses skepticism about the whole:

> Mallarmé had just written *L'Après-midi d'un faune* and wanted his eclogue (which was to be performed at this short-lived theater [Théâtre des Arts]) set to music and sung, quite like a little opera. The poet therefore asked his friend Hérold to present Debussy for this purpose. The meeting took place at Hérold's home, and, I believe I remember correctly, in the presence of Pierre Louÿs. Debussy accepted the proposal of Mallarmé and went to work. The Théâtre des Arts closed shop and the score remained unfinished. But even incomplete it was extant. Hérold saw it (Debussy played him fragments from it), he told me.[17]

It was in 1891 also that Mallarmé told the interviewer Jules Huret that in the *Faun* he had tried "to make a sort of running pianistic commentary upon the . . . alexandrine." [18] The meaning of this fanciful remark can be guessed at only on the basis of many other statements.

17. Jean Dupérier, *Découverte du vieux monde: lettres d'un musicien ambulant à un confrère sédentaire,* Paris, 1957, p. 186 ff. Not mentioned by Lockspeiser, this item came to my attention through a brief article by Marc Pincherle in *Nouvelles littéraires,* October 4, 1962.

18. See below, p. 111.

In the same year the young Valéry wrote to Mallarmé to express his enormous admiration of the *Faun:*

> The supreme idea is now gaining ground of a lofty symphony uniting the world around us with the inner world that haunts us, constructed according to a strict architecture, putting an end to the simplified types labeled with gold and blue, and liberating the poet from the burdensome aid of banal philosophies, of false tendernesses, of lifeless descriptions. In France this esthetic ideal is realized only by *L'Après-midi du [sic] faune.*[19]

Mallarmé in his reply, May 5, 1891, testified:

> Such a poem is suggested by music proper, which we must raid and paraphrase, if our own music, struck dumb, is insufficient.[20]

In the next six years Mallarmé developed this notion much farther, discussed it at length, and exemplified it in his last works, which make the *Faun* seem almost conventional and easy.

In 1892 Debussy knew Mallarmé well enough to invite a new friend and patron, Prince André Poniatowski, to Mallarmé's Tuesday evenings.[21] Early in their acquaintance, according to Poniatowski, Debussy took him and Mallarmé to hear Gregorian chant sung at the Church of St. Gervais, where Charles Bordes was conductor. Mallarmé's article on this visit, published May 7, 1892, tells of polyphonic choral music and an organ postlude.[22]

In the summer of 1892, Debussy bought a copy of the newly published play by Maurice Maeterlinck, *Pelléas et Mélisande.* On May 17, 1893, when the play was performed in Paris, both Debussy and Mallarmé attended. Debussy was already at work transforming it into his one completed opera (essentially completed in 1895, first performed in 1902). Mallarmé wrote a laudatory review of the play.

In view of all this, we may reasonably imagine that the poet and composer together discussed the *Faun* and various possibilities of music connected with the poem.

1892 seems to have been the year in which Debussy began most of the major projects that he completed in the following years. Besides the

---

19. Paul Valéry, *Lettres à quelques-uns,* Paris, 1952, p. 47. See also his *Écrits divers sur Stéphane Mallarmé,* Paris, 1950.
20. Henri Mondor, *Propos familiers de Paul Valéry,* Paris, 1957, p. 147.
21. André Poniatowski, *D'un siècle à l'autre,* Paris, 1948.
22. Mallarmé, *Solennités,* in *National Observer,* May 7, 1892; reprinted under the heading *De même* in his *Divagations* and found on p. 395 in the Pléiade edition of his *Œuvres complètes,* ed. by Mondor (Paris, 1945).

biggest of all, *Pelléas,* and the one that concerns us continually here, the *Faun,* there was the String Quartet, finished in February, 1893; the Nocturnes for orchestra, 1899; the first set of three Verlaine songs entitled *Fêtes galantes,* finished in 1892 though not published until 1903; and the four songs on texts by Debussy himself, *Proses lyriques,* finished 1893, published 1895. It appears that somehow Debussy had made a fundamental choice that released his energy to carry things through to completion, though he was still far from working according to any routine and his later career is as full of unfinished projects as were the years before this turning point. If it is true that there was a fundamental decision, we may speculate further that the ideas of Mallarmé contributed something essential to it. Although Godet reported in 1929 that Debussy "never breathed a word" to him about Mallarmé,[23] Lockspeiser concludes from the testimonies of Louÿs, Poniatowski, and others that their relation was close. The chronology, as we have reviewed it here, tends to confirm Lockspeiser's view. Yet surely Debussy was no mere disciple of Mallarmé, or translator of his ideas into the language of music. We may note from a letter of Debussy to Chausson, 1893,[24] that Mallarmé's late works stirred him to opposition as well as admiration.

The evidence that Debussy began the *Faun* in 1892 is the presence of that date on his manuscript, finished in 1894. But in 1892 the idea may have been still quite vague. Two public announcements in 1893 and even 1894 indicate that the *Prelude* we know was only part of the vague idea. The cover of *La Damoiselle élue,* published shortly after its first performance in April, 1893 (in an edition of 160 copies with a drawing by Maurice Denis), listed a forthcoming work as *Prélude, interludes et paraphrase finale pour l'Après-midi d'un faune.* The same title appeared on the program of an all-Debussy concert in Brussels, March 1, 1894, but no such piece was played then. Thus we may guess that Debussy pondered the work a long time, inventing much more than he ultimately used.

The year 1893 was so eventful for Debussy that we can hardly guess when he found time for the *Faun.* In February the Quartet was finished. In April the *Damoiselle* was performed. In May Debussy played illustrations for a public lecture by Mendès on the *Ring.* In the summer he composed at least one scene of *Pelléas,* and in the fall he went to Ghent with Louÿs to call on Maeterlinck and obtain his permission to use the

23. *Revue musicale,* VII (1926), 71.
24. See below, p. 136.

play for his opera. But by September 6 he had composed the *Faun*, at least in his head, because that day he reported to Chausson that he had played it through for their mutual friend, the poet Régnier. In December Debussy and his mistress moved into an attic room on the Rue Gustave-Doré. At the end of December there was the first performance of the Quartet, at the Société Nationale; this firmly established Debussy's reputation among French musicians, including Saint-Saëns's pupil Gabriel Fauré (1845–1924), though it disappointed Chausson, for whom Debussy promised to write a second, better quartet.

The year 1894 was similarly crowded. But by October 23 the *Faun* was complete in full score and reduction for two pianos; on this day Debussy signed the receipt for 200 francs from Hartmann, assigning him all rights in the composition.[25] The concert in Brussels in March, the publication of the Quartet in the fall, the composition of four piano pieces, some two-piano arrangements of music by Schumann and Saint-Saëns, and continuing progress on the Nocturnes and *Pelléas* must have left little time for the *Faun*. But parts were copied soon enough for ample rehearsals before the concerts of the Société Nationale on December 22 and 23. The performance was judged a great success by its conductor, Gustave Doret (1866–1943).[26]

Two days before the performance, Debussy wrote to Mallarmé in an ironic style worthy of the poet—though not, according to Henri Mondor, immaculately spelled and punctuated:

> Cher maître
> Need I tell you what joy I shall have if you will be so kind as to indulge with your presence the arabesques which I have been led to believe, through a pride perhaps reprehensible, were inspired by the flute of your Faun?
> Yours very respectfully,
> Claude Debussy [27]

Mallarmé's reaction to the concert, in a letter to Debussy cited only as a fragment by Léon Vallas, was precisely expressed:

> .... your illustration of *L'Après-midi d'un faune* would present no dissonance with my text, unless to go further, indeed, into the nostaglia and the light, with finesse, with malaise, with richness.[28]

25. Reproduction of this letter in Barraqué, *Debussy*, Paris, 1962, p. 93.
26. See below, p. 138.
27. Cited by Mondor, *L'Histoire d'un faun*, p. 273, and Lockspeiser, I, 156.
28. Léon Vallas, *Claude Debussy et son temps*, rev. ed., Paris, 1958, p. 180. Mondor, *op. cit.*, p. 272, apparently copies Vallas's fragment.

Long afterward, in 1910, Debussy responded to an inquiry from Jean-Aubry with his recollection of Mallarmé's earlier and later reactions to the music:

> ... I was living then in a little furnished apartment on the Rue de Londres. [If Debussy's memory was correct, this dates the occasion before late 1893, when he moved to the Rue Gustave-Doré.] ... Mallarmé came in, with his Sybilline look and wearing a Scotch plaid. After having listened, he was silent for a long time, and then said to me: "I was not expecting anything of this kind! This music prolongs the emotion of my poem, and sets its scene more vividly than color."
> And here is the verse that Mallarmé inscribed on the copy of *L'Après-midi d'un faune* that he sent me after the first performance:
>
> > O forest god of breathing air,
> > If you have made your flute aright,
> > Now hear the way that Debussy
> > Breathes into it the broad daylight.
>
> This is a first-rate document for whoever is concerned!
> In any case, it is my happiest memory from this period, when I was not yet bothered with "Debussysme." [29]

In the following spring and summer Debussy was occupied again with *Pelléas*, but the *Faun* was not forgotten. On July 3, 1895, he signed a well-thumbed copy of the score—perhaps the one used by Doret—pointing out to the engraver three misprints.[30] On October 9 he wrote to Louÿs that he was terribly busy with rehearsals for performances of the *Faun* under the direction of Edouard Colonne, which took place on two successive Sundays, October 13 and 20. On October 17 Debussy sent Louÿs a copy of the score, inscribed "A few flute tunes to charm Bilitis"—an allusion to the new poems of Louÿs from which Debussy was soon to choose some for songs and some others for the pieces that eventually became the *Épigraphes antiques*. On October 10 Debussy wrote to his friend the journalist Henri Gauthier-Villars, who evidently had sought material for his newspaper report of the Colonne concert:

> The *Prélude à "L'Après-midi d'un faune,"* dear Sir, might it be what remains of the dream at the tip of the faun's flute? More precisely, it is a general impression of the poem, for if music were to follow more closely it would run out of breath, like a dray horse competing for the Grand Prize with a thoroughbred. There is also [my] scorn for

---

29. Debussy, *Lettres à deux amis*, Paris, 1942, p. 121.
30. This copy is now in the Sibley Library, Eastman School of Music, Rochester, New York.

that eager-beaver learning that weighs down our proudest brains. And then there is no reverence for the key! Rather it is in a mode that tries to contain all the shadings, which is very logically demonstrable. Now still, all of it does follow the rising movement of the poem. And there is the scenery, marvelously described in the text, with, furthermore, the humanity contributed by thirty-two violinists who had to get up too early! The end is the last line prolonged:

Couple, good-bye! To see the shadow you become, I go.[31]

Léon Vallas, who quotes this letter in his biography of Debussy, quotes also a more conventional "note," perhaps for the Colonne concert-program, which Debussy himself either wrote or at least approved:

> The music of this *Prelude* is a very free illustration of the beautiful poem of Mallarmé. By no means does it claim to be a synthesis of the latter. Rather there are the successive scenes through which pass the desires and dreams of the faun in the heat of this afternoon. Then, tired of pursuing the fearful flight of the nymphs and the naiads, he succumbs to intoxicating sleep, in which he can finally realize his dreams of possession in universal Nature.[32]

Colonne's performance was reviewed in various journals of 1895. Vallas quotes from several of these reviews, including the most extensive one, by Gustave Robert.[33] Another, which Vallas neglects, may be cited here, since it appeared in the *Mercure de France,* an organ of Mallarmé's disciples. The reviewer was the young poet Charles-Henry Hirsch. After mentioning various opinions of the music among those who had heard it the previous season at the Salle d'Harcourt, Hirsch gave his considered judgment:

> To us the truth seems that this musician, if he is not quite gifted with an abundant inspiration, knows marvelously the resources of his art, and that the *Prélude à "L'Après-midi d'un faune"* is a symphonic picture full of novelty. The charm it exerts is really great, and there is a rare pleasure in following this description, where, in the development of a motif, incidental fragments arise that animate the scene in the most felicitous way. And there is a close connection uniting the composition of M. Debussy with the magificent poem of M. Stéphane Mallarmé.[34]

One other review claims special interest, because it evoked a comment from Debussy. This was the report in *Le Figaro* by the prominent com-

---

31. Vallas, *op. cit.,* p. 181.
32. *Ibid.,* p. 181. This note is printed with the Eulenberg edition of the Prelude, where its source is said to be "the original edition."
33. See below, p. 147.
34. C.-H. Hirsch, *Musique,* in *Mercure de France,* XVI (1895), 255.

poser Alfred Bruneau (1857–1934), who praised the originality and exquisite refinement of the work, although confessing that he preferred "an art more clear, more robust, more masculine." Debussy wrote to Bruneau on October 17, 1895:

> My dear friend,
> Accept my warm thanks for the fine article devoted to the *Prelude* . . . and also for the example of artistic fraternity that you give there. This is what should be praised in those who, like you, allow for an art other than their own.[35]

In November, 1895, Debussy sent Mallarmé a copy of his score.[36] Only now, perhaps, with the work publicly launched and recognized, was Debussy ready to see it enshrined in the poet's library.

Later in the fall of 1895 there was still another performance of the *Faun*, this one conducted by André Messager. More performances followed, so many, indeed, that by 1899, when Debussy was ready to introduce his *Nocturnes*, he protested Hartmann's proposal that the *Faun* be played on the same program; a letter of September 24, 1899, demands:

> Do you think it is really useful to play *"L'Après-midi d'un faune"* before the Nocturnes? That seems to me to be turning into an obsession —to the faun made permanent! [37]

Meanwhile, in 1895, Mallarmé had published his important lecture on *Music and Literature*, delivered at Oxford and Cambridge the year before.[38] Did Debussy read it? There is no evidence. In 1896 Mallarmé collected his prose writings for publication with the title *Divagations*. The event was celebrated at a ceremonial dinner, which Debussy attended, February 2, 1897. On February 9 he wrote about it to Louÿs:

> You should be informed of all that should be known about the Mallarmé banquet? I was prodigiously bored. Mallarmé seemed to share my reaction, and he gave, in a voice of puppet-like melancholy, a brief discourse, coldly irritated. . . .[39]

Later in 1897 Mallarmé's most original work appeared, *Un Coup de dés*

---

35. This unpublished letter, in the Bibliothèque Nationale, Paris, was called to my attention by M. François Lesure. For Bruneau's review, see below, p. 145.
36. This copy was exhibited at the Bibliothèque Nationale in 1962. See the catalogue of the exhibition: François Lesure, ed., *Claude Debussy*, Paris, 1962, p. 38.
37. Debussy, *Lettres inédites*, in *Revue musicale*, 258 (1964), 113.
38. See below, p. 112.
39. Debussy and Louÿs, *Correspondance*, p. 87.

(A Throw of Dice), which his preface described as a combination of free verse and prose-poem:

> Their union is achieved under an admittedly foreign influence, that of Music heard at the concert; here one rediscovers several means that have seemed to me to belong to Letters; I reclaim them.[40]

The next year Mallarmé died. Valéry, sending word to Louÿs, added, "Tell Debussy."

After *Pelléas* began to make Debussy famous abroad, the *Faun* was the first of his orchestral works to be performed in many cities. Among noteworthy performances were these:

April, 1902, Boston, conducted by Georges Longy (who had learned the piece as oboist under Colonne in 1895)
November, 1903, Berlin, Ferruccio Busoni
1904, London, Henry Wood
March, 1906, Turin, Arturo Toscanini
December, 1907, Vienna, Richard Strauss.

Still later Debussy himself appeared on the podium—somewhat unwillingly and by most reports ineffectively— to conduct the *Faun*. Among those appearances, the following are interesting:

February, 1908 and again February, 1909, London
December, 1910, Vienna
June, 1911, Turin
April, 1913, Paris, for the opening of the new Théâtre des Champs Élysées.

The copy of the score that Debussy possessed during these years contains numerous pencil markings of nuances and tempi, probable traces of his conducting experience. This precious score, now in the library of François Lang at Royaumont, has been a principal source for the present edition.

In 1912 the Ballets Russes, in Paris since 1909, presented a new incarnation of the faun, which became almost as famous as the music or the poem, and doubtless considerably increased the fame of both. Despite many incongruities noted by critics at the time and ever since, the dance provided associations that clung to the music in many minds.[41] The

40. Mallarmé, *Œuvres complètes*, Paris, 1961, p. 455.
41. For a careful consideration of the associations, see Thomas Munro, "*The Afternoon of a Faun*" and the Interrelation of the Arts, in *Journal of Aesthetics and Art Criticism*, X (1951), 95; reprinted in his collected essays, *Toward Science in Aesthetics*, New York, 1956, p. 342.

dancer Vaslav Nijinsky was the brightest star of Serge Diaghilev's company—one of the greatest performers of any age—and with the *Faun,* his first essay in choreography, he proved to be also a revolutionary creative artist. But he did not especially like Debussy's music. Something more stark and archaic-sounding would have suited better the friezelike notion of the poem that Nijinsky and Diaghilev realized, with a row of six girls as foil for Nijinsky himself. Nevertheless, drawings and photographs of him in the spotted faun costume designed by Léon Bakst are unforgettable. They can only be counteracted by some different picture. An etching of a faun's head by Odilon Redon, for instance, may make us regret that Diaghilev failed in his effort to have Redon design the sets and costumes.[42] (Debussy had probably known Redon as a friend of Chausson; he certainly knew his work, and possibly attended the first exhibition of it in the year of his own *Faun,* 1894. On the other hand, Redon's public praise of Nijinsky's *Faun* did not endear him to Debussy.) For Americans of the second half of the twentieth-century, the altogether new interpretation by Jerome Robbins (1953), which substitutes a sober ballet studio for the sylvan scene and has only one ballerina to figure forth the one male dancer's inspiration, may be the most appropriate picture to go with the music.

Nijinsky's *Faun* had coincidental effects that delayed full appreciation of the classic quality of Debussy's music. The great notoriety of the ballet and the special exertions of the company to produce it [43] marred the success of at least two other new works in the same season: Ravel's *Daphnis et Chloë,* with choreography by Fokine, and Reynaldo Hahn's *Dieu bleu,* with scenario by Jean Cocteau. Ravel and Fokine were lost to Diaghilev's future enterprises, which they might well have ennobled with works even greater than any they had the chance to compose. Cocteau, at the very beginning of his theatrical career, was to turn away from Hahn toward Satie and Picasso and others, with whom he would provide for Diaghilev a whole series of shocking surprises. Cocteau and his friends rose to fame by the contrast their works made with Debussy's, and by their polemical interpretation of his work as old-fashioned and sentimental. In a pamphlet, *Cock and Harlequin,* which appeared in the year Debussy died (1918), Cocteau exercised his witty ingenuity to praise Satie at the expense of Debussy:

---

42. Ari Redon, ed., *Lettres . . . à Odilon Redon,* Paris, 1960, p. 228.
43. Sergei Leonidovich Grigoriev, *The Diaghilev Ballet 1909–1929,* trans. V. Bowen, London, 1953, p. 61 ff.

> Debussy enthrones the Debussy climate once and for all. Satie transforms himself. . . . Debussy fell from the German frying-pan into the Russian fire. Once more the pedal blurs the rhythm, makes a sort of misty climate, favorable to short-sighted ears. . . . You can get lost in Debussy's mist as you can in Wagner's heavy fog.

This propaganda got Satie talked about more than played. It was more practically helpful to the young friends of Satie and Cocteau: Milhaud, Honegger, and Poulenc. To be sure, it did not stop Debussy from being played (nor did it stop Milhaud, Honegger, or Poulenc from loving and studying Debussy's work), but it probably encouraged many "short-sighted listeners" to let their minds wander in the alleged mist, instead of listening to Debussy with the full alertness that the newest music more obviously demanded. The lazy-minded of the 1920s and '30s thought of Debussy as a belated minor offshoot of the romantic era, remote from the concerns of Milhaud, not to mention Schoenberg or Stravinsky. Cocteau, by no means lazy-minded himself, often acknowledged the grandeur of Debussy and the deliberate injustice of his own attack. As early as 1923, in his public letter to Jacques Maritain, he explained, "In 1916, to my deep regret, I had to seem as if I were attacking Debussy. In reality I was attacking Debussyism." [45] Again, when Cocteau reviewed a book by Debussy's friend and biographer Louis Laloy (1928), he looked back generously:

> In 1922 he [Laloy] was my enemy and the enemy of the young musicians because his exclusive friendship for Claude Debussy made him suppose that our arbitrary, unjust, expedient antidotes (we had to take short-cuts) were insulting the work that we cherish, the work whose place is so secure that it withstands any attack.[46]

But these tributes never quite caught up with the attack. To define and secure the place of Debussy's work in the history of music was the task of many younger writers, and more especially of musicians whose writing could be reinforced by their performances of Debussy's music and by new compositions that acknowledged its influence. Chief among such musicians is Pierre Boulez. He and his friends, the pioneers of electronic music Herbert Eimert and Karlheinz Stockhausen, beginning in 1954,

---

44. Jean Cocteau, *Le Coq et l'arlequin*. Paris, 1918, pp. 27, 26, and 41 respectively.
45. Cocteau and Maritain, *Art and Faith*, trans. John Coleman, New York, 1948, p. 69.
46. Cocteau, *Œuvres complètes*, Geneva, 1946–51, X, 332.

cited Debussy's ballet *Jeux* as a seminal work for their enterprise.[47] In 1958 Boulez surveyed Debussy's whole career in the light of young composers' concerns; he discussed the *Faun* as a landmark, the beginning of "modern music."[48] This tribute may arouse the skepticism of some conservative musicians of the 1960s; is Boulez merely swinging the pendulum in the opposite direction from that of Cocteau? No, in the opinion of the present writer, Boulez is right, and a somewhat detailed consideration of the "formal liberty" and "sonorous balance" in the *Faun* can reinforce his high estimate of Debussy's achievement.

47. Pierre Boulez, *Debussy: "Jeux,"* in *Gravesaner Blätter*, 2/3 (1956), 5; Karlheinz Stockhausen, *Texte*, Cologne, 1963, I, p. 75; Herbert Eimert, *Debussy's "Jeux,"* in *Die Reihe* (English ed.), V (1961), 3.
48. See below, p. 160.

The Text of Mallarmé's Poem

Translating the poem into English risks the breathlessness that Debussy said would afflict any attempt at a literal musical "translation." English does seem like a dray horse competing with the thoroughbred French. But the effort is fascinating, and sometimes helpful as a means of appreciating the poem. Roger Fry, who translated all Mallarmé's poems, recommended that "like the Bible he should be translated by a Committee" (Mallarmé, *Poems,* trans. by Roger Fry, New York, 1937, p. 308). There is a translation of the *Faun* by one great English writer, Aldous Huxley, which sacrifices some of the literal sense in order to make a continuity of rhythm—pentameter corresponding to the classic French alexandrines —and even of rhyme (Huxley, *The Defeat of Youth, and Other Poems,* Oxford, 1918, p. 44). The following compromise owes much to both Fry and Huxley. It owes something, moreover, to the early French versions (1865 and 1875), where the literal sense is occasionally clearer than it became in the final one (1876), the only one used by Fry and Huxley. Readers are invited to join the "committee" and improve on this version. Better than that, they are invited to use it as a prelude to Debussy's *Prelude*—as an indirect way of discovering more and more of what he discovered in Mallarmé.

L'Après-midi d'un faune

Églogue
par Stéphane Mallarmé

LE FAUNE

Ces nymphes, je les veux perpétuer.

                         Si clair,
Leur incarnat léger, qu'il voltige dans l'air
Assoupi de sommeils touffus.

                        Aimai-je un rêve?

Mon doute, amas de nuit ancienne, s'achève
En maint rameau subtil, qui, demeuré les vrais
Bois mêmes, prouve, hélas! que bien seul je m'offrais
Pour triomphe la faute idéale de roses—

Réfléchissons . . .

              ou si les femmes dont tu gloses
Figurent un souhait de tes sens fabuleux!
Faune, l'illusion s'échappe des yeux bleus
Et froids, comme une source en pleurs, de la plus chaste:
Mais, l'autre tout soupirs, dis-tu qu'elle contraste
Comme brise du jour chaude dans ta toison?
Que non! par l'immobile et lasse pâmoison
Suffoquant de chaleurs le matin frais s'il lutte,
Ne murmure point d'eau que ne verse ma flûte
Au bosquet arrosé d'accords; et le seul vent

The Afternoon of a Faun

Eclogue
by Stéphane Mallarmé

THE FAUN

Those nymphs, I want to make them permanent.

                                        So clear
Their light flesh-pink, it hovers on the atmosphere
Oppressed by bushy sleeps.

                  Was it a dream I loved?

My doubt, accumulated through the night past, branches out
To many a fine point—no more in fact than twigs—
Proving, alas! that what I'd claimed for trophy, by myself,
Was only my imagination's lack of roses.

Let's think . . .

                might not the girls you are describing be
Wishful figments of your mythopoetic senses?
Faun, your illusion flies from that shy girl's blue eyes,
Cool as a weeping spring: the other one, all sighs—
Does she make, say, a contrast like today's faint breeze,
Warm on your fleece? Oh, no! this enervating swoon
Of heat, which stifles all fresh dawn's resistance,
Allows no splash of water but that which my flute
Pours into chord-besprinkled thickets; as for breeze—

Hors des deux tuyaux prompt à s'exhaler avant
Qu'il disperse le son dans une pluie aride,
C'est, à l'horizon pas remué d'une ride,
Le visible et serein souffle artificiel
De l'inspiration, qui regagne le ciel.

O bords siciliens d'un calme marécage
Qu'à l'envi des soleils ma vanité saccage,
Tacites sous les fleurs d'étincelles, CONTEZ
"Que je coupais ici les creux roseaux domptés
"Par le talent; quand, sur l'or glauque de lointaines
"Verdures dédiant leur vigne à des fontaines,
"Ondoie une blancheur animale au repos:
"Et qu'au prélude lent où naissent les pipeaux,
"Ce vol de cygnes, non! de naïades se sauve
"Ou plonge . . .
                  Inerte, tout brûle dans l'heure fauve
Sans marquer par quel art ensemble détala
Trop d'hymen souhaité de qui cherche le *la:*
Alors m'éveillerais-je à la ferveur première,
Droit et seul, sous un flot antique de lumière,
Lys! et l'un de vous tous pour ingénuité.

Autre que ce doux rien par leur lèvre ébruité,
Le baiser, qui tout bas des perfides assure,
Mon sein, vierge de preuve, atteste une morsure
Mystérieuse, due à quelque auguste dent;
Mais, bast! arcane tel élut pour confident
Le jonc vaste et jumeau dont sous l'azur on joue:
Qui, détournant à soi le trouble de la joue,
Rêve, dans un solo long, que nous amusions
La beauté d'alentour par des confusions
Fausses entre elle-même et notre chant crédule;
Et de faire aussi haut que l'amour se module
Évanouir du songe ordinaire de dos
Ou de flanc pur suivis avec mes regards clos,
Une sonore, vaine et monotone ligne.

The Afternoon of a Faun

Except for my two pipes, blown empty long before
It could have scattered notes in parching rain—the only
Breeze is, out there on the immaculate horizon,
The visible, serene, and calculated breath
Of inspiration, as it is drawn back to heaven.

You still Sicilian marsh's fringes, which my vain
Reflection, like the sunbeams, spoils, do not remain
Silent beneath their flowery glintings; rather TELL:
    "Here I was cutting hollow reeds, won by my skill,
    When over the dull gold of distant arbors, with
    Their vines devotedly entwining fountains, floats
    A live whiteness at rest: now with the slow prelude
    In which the pipes warm up, this flight of swans—I mean,
    Of Naiads—evanesces or goes under . . ."
                                      Passive,
The whole scene burns in this fierce hour without a sign
Of what craft whisked away the wished-for nuptial
As I tune up my A: so that I wake again
To warmth, just as before, erect, alone,
Under a long familiar wave of light, O lilies!
With one of you to compensate my innocence.

Quite unlike that sweet nothing by their lip divulged,
The kiss, that softly reassures unfaithful lovers,
My breast, though virginal of proof, betrays a mystery—
The bite of some proud tooth. But hush! whatever
The secret was, it chose for its safe vehicle
The spacious double reed I play under the blue,
Which, taking to itself my cheek's hot agitation,
Dreams in a long soliloquy that we did entertain
The beauty all around us by deceitfully
Confusing it with that of our credulous song;
And further that we might, no matter how high love
May be transposed, distill from vulgar thought of shoulder
Or thigh, which I pursue with leering scrutiny,
A single line of sound, aloof, disinterested.

Tâche donc, instrument des fuites, ô maligne
Syrinx, de refleurir aux lacs où tu m'attends!
Moi, de ma rumeur fier, je vais parler longtemps
Des déesses; et, par d'idolâtres peintures,
A leur ombre enlever encore des ceintures:
Ainsi, quand des raisins j'ai sucé la clarté,
Pour bannir un regret par ma feinte écarté,
Rieur, j'élève au ciel d'été la grappe vide
Et, soufflant dans ses peaux lumineuses, avide
D'ivresse, jusqu'au soir je regarde au travers.

O nymphes, regonflons des SOUVENIRS divers.
"Mon œil, trouant les joncs, dardait chaque encolure
"Immortelle, qui noie en l'onde sa brûlure
"Avec un cri de rage au ciel de la forêt;
"Et le splendide bain de cheveux disparaît
"Dans les clartés et les frissons, ô pierreries!
"J'accours; quand, à mes pieds, s'entrejoignent (meurtries
"De la langueur goûtée à ce mal d'être deux)
"Des dormeuses parmi leurs seuls bras hasardeux:
"Je les ravis, sans les désenlacer, et vole
"A ce massif, haï par l'ombrage frivole,
"De roses tarissant tout parfum au soleil,
"Où notre ébat au jour consumé soit pareil.
Je t'adore, courroux des vierges, ô délice
Farouche du sacré fardeau nu qui se glisse
Pour fuir ma lèvre en feu buvant, comme un éclair
Tressaille! la frayeur secrète de la chair:
Des pieds de l'inhumaine au cœur de la timide
Que délaisse à la fois une innocence, humide
De larmes folles ou de moins tristes vapeurs.
"Mon crime, c'est d'avoir, gai de vaincre ces peurs
"Traîtresses, divisé la touffe échevelée
"De baisers que les dieux gardaient si bien mêlée;
"Car, à peine j'allais cacher un rire ardent
"Sous les replis heureux d'une seule (gardant
"Par un doigt simple, afin que sa candeur de plume
"Se teignît à l'émoi de sa sœur qui s'allume,

The Afternoon of a Faun

Syrinx, sly elusive instrument, go try
To bloom again beside the pools where you await me!
Proud of my noise, now I shall speak at length about
The goddesses; and so, by means of sacrilegious
Paintings, undress them in their shadow.
Likewise, when I have sucked the sweetness out of grapes,
In order to put off regret by harmless trickery,
I laugh and lift the empty bunch to summer sky
And puffing into all the shiny skins, insatiable
For drunkenness, I gaze through them till evening.

O nymphs, let's resurrect our various MEMORIES.
    "My eye, piercing the rushes, found its target in
    Each superhuman throat that in the wave has drowned
    Its heat, crying with fury to the jungle sky.
    Even the glowing bath of hair must vanish
    In brightnesses and rippling thrills, O jewels!
    I run closer; now at my feet lie interlocked
    (Felled by the languid misery of being two)
    Girls sleeping, with their reckless arms around each other.
    I take them, without separating them, and fly
    To this enclosure, which all futile shade avoids,
    Drying the scent of roses in the sun, that we
    May play a game resembling the exhausted day."
O holy wrath of virgins! I adore you, O
Wild tang of lovely naked burdens gliding to
Evade my fiery lip that sucks as thrilling as
Lightning! the secret creeping of the flesh:
From cruel sister's foot to timid sister's heart
Let innocence abandon both at once; wet it
With silly tears, or else with moistures not so sad.
    "My crime was this: in my delight at conquering
    Those treacherous fears, I did divide the casual bunch
    Of kisses that the gods kept so well mixed;
    For hardly had I hidden an exulting laugh
    Under the blessed folds of one of them (keeping my touch
    By just a finger—so her feathery whiteness might
    Be colored by her sister's kindling passion—with

"La petite, naïve et ne rougissant pas:)
"Que de mes bras, défaits par de vagues trépas,
"Cette proie, à jamais ingrate, se délivre
"Sans pitié du sanglot dont j'étais encore ivre.

Tant pis! vers le bonheur d'autres m'entraîneront
Par leur tresse nouée aux cornes de mon front:
Tu sais, ma passion, que, pourpre et déjà mûre,
Chaque grenade éclate et d'abeilles murmure;
Et notre sang, épris de qui le va saisir,
Coule pour tout l'essaim éternel du désir.
A l'heure où ce bois d'or et de cendres se teinte
Une fête s'exalte en la feuillée éteinte:
Etna! c'est parmi toi visité de Vénus
Sur ta lave posant ses talons ingénus,
Quand tonne un somme triste ou s'épuise la flamme.

Je tiens la reine!

    O sûr châtiment . . .

     Non, mais l'âme
De paroles vacante et ce corps allourdi
Tard succombent au fier silence de midi:
Sans plus il faut dormir en l'oubli du blasphème,
Sur la sable altéré gisant et comme j'aime
Ouvrir ma bouche à l'astre efficace des vins!

Couple, adieu; je vais voir l'ombre que tu devins.

The Afternoon of a Faun

The naïve little one who was not blushing yet)
When from my arms, relaxed by quasi-deaths, my prey,
Always ungrateful, slips away, pitiless toward
My gasp of gluttonous intoxication."

Ah well, too bad! Toward happiness there will be others
To draw me on by their hair caught up on my horns.
You know, my libido, that every pomegranate
When it grows ripe and red must burst and buzz with bees;
Just so our blood, stirred by someone about to grasp it,
Will flow for all the endless hive of appetite.
At twilight when this wood turns gold and gray a rite
Is celebrated in the dying foliage:
Along your slope, O Etna! visited by Venus,
Who treads your lava with her harmless heels when sad
Sleep rumbles or the final flame goes flickering out.

I hold the queen!

                Oh, certain punishment . . .

No, but my speechless soul and heavy-laden body
Succumb at last to noontime's ceremonial pause.
Now I must simply nap, forget my blasphemy,
Stretching my legs on rumpled sand, and happily
Must yawn at yonder star that keeps vines growing!

Couple, good-bye; to see the shadow you become I'm going.

The Score of Debussy's Prelude

INSTRUMENTATION

3 Flutes (Fl.)
2 Oboes (Hautb.)
1 English Horn (Cor Angl.)
2 Clarinets (Cl.), in A (La) and B♭ (Si♭)
2 Bassoons (Bons.)
4 Horns (Cors) in F
2 Harps (Harpes)
Antique Cymbals (Cymb. Ant.)
Violin I (1rs. Vns.)
Violin II (2ds. Vns.)
Viola (Altos)
Cello (Vlles.)
Double Bass

PRELUDE TO
"THE AFTERNOON OF A FAUN"

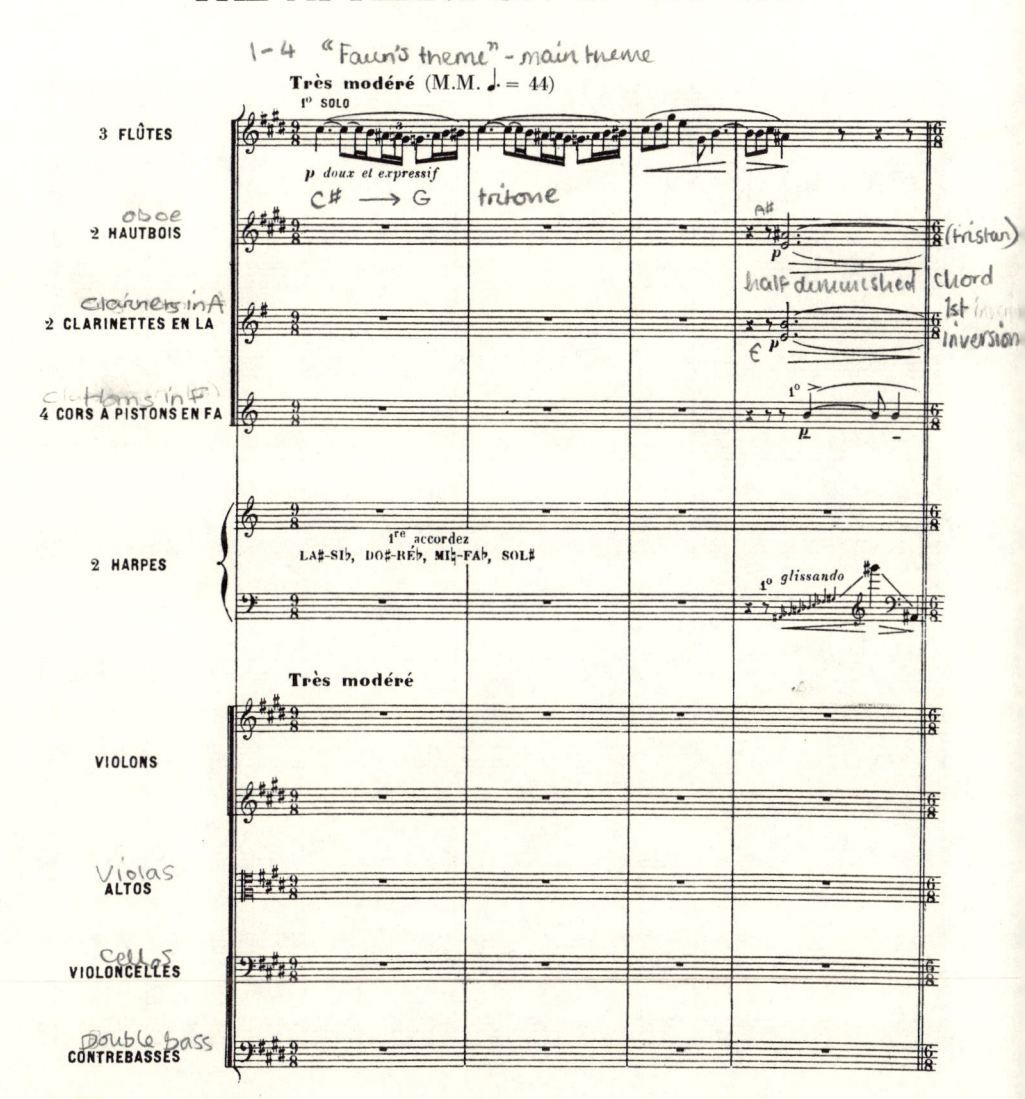

Debussy

Prelude to "The Afternoon of a Faun"

36 — Debussy

Several entries of the main theme, various modifications
2
21
E major chord C# 6th added
1re FL.
SOLO
légèrement et expressif
"Fauns theme" First note extended + elaborated
Syncopated motif
2o
CORS
4o
1re HARPE
2e HARPE
Prominent gesture
low String accomp
Div.
pizz.

38 Transformed Main theme Debussy
transposed major 3rd down

perfect 4th instead of tritone

B9 chord (dom 7th + maj 9th)

major 9th

E9 chord

Prelude to "The Afternoon of a Faun"

28
"floating motive"
"syncopated motive"
Cédez . . .
Perfect cadence
V
FL.
Bons
1o tr
Cédez . . .
Div.
Unis
Unis
dim.
dim.
Div.
dim.
Div.
arco
30
in
I BMaj
31
3
au Mouvt
acceleration of main gesture from 'Fauns' theme
1re FL.
CL
Clarinet = change in timbre
1o
sourdines
CORS
sourdines
Horns
accomp.
Chord based on whole tone scale
1re HARPE
au Mouvt
ôtez vite les sourdines
ôtez vite les sourdines
ôtez vite les sourdines
Celli–counterpoint
new motive
pizz.

Prelude to "The Afternoon of a Faun"

41

Debussy

Prelude to "The Afternoon of a Faun"

Debussy

Prelude to "The Afternoon of a Faun"

46   Debussy

54
Cédez un peu . . .
55
Même mouvt et très soutenu (M.M. ♩= 56)
p expressif et très soutenu
mf
Fl.
Hautb.
Cor angl.
Cl.
Bons
Cors
(3. 4.)
pp
Même mouvt et très soutenu
arco
chorus theme - smooth transition
approach to next climax
tutti
woodwinds present 'chorus' theme
new
alternates
Db maj
whole tone chord
Prominent tritone
Db → G

7
59
61
Tutti forte
MAIN CLIMAX OF THE PIECE
'floating motive' in A minor
CRESC
FL.
2° et 3°
HAUTB.
à 2
COR ANGL.
CL.
Bons
1°
CORS
1.2.
3.4.
4°
cresc
cre - - - scen - - - do
più f
Unis
Div.

→ relative major
Strings
'CHORUS'
theme
(Db maj)
63–66

Db → G

tritone in bass
Same harmony as
'floating motive'

50   *Debussy*

Prelude to "The Afternoon of a Faun"

Gb maj theme of sonority

Climax fades away
decresc, orchestra reduced
72
74
Cédez un peu
(M.M. ♩= 60)
FL.
CL.
1°
'floating motive' - clarinets + oboes
p très doux
Bons
p espressif et doux
CORS
'Syncopated' motive transferred to horn
1re HARPE
Violin solo back to 'chorus' theme
Vons SOLO
Cédez un peu . .
p doux et expressif
sourdines
Div.

Prelude to "The Afternoon of a Faun" 53

Debussy

Prelude to "The Afternoon of a Faun"

56 *Transposition of bars 79-85 a minor 2nd lower*   *Debussy*

9 **86**

*main theme in oboe instead of flute
Eb major*

Prelude to "The Afternoon of a Faun"

58   Debussy

Prelude to "The Afternoon of a Faun"   59

Debussy

Prelude to "The Afternoon of a Faun"

11
102
Retenu
103
(a tempo)
Très retenu
1er FL.
HAUTB.
1°
SOLO
COR ANGL.
CL.
Bons
CORS
2°
(sourdines)
Retenu
(a tempo)
Très retenu
extension of theme in Flute
C maj7 - 2nd part of theme
Second part of main theme
divisi strings

Prelude to "The Afternoon of a Faun"

Textual Note

Sources used for the present edition are as follows:

J Manuscript score, conveyed from Debussy to the publisher Hartmann on October 23, 1894; now in the archive of Editions Jobert, Paris. Mme. Jobert-Georges, director general of the company, provided the present editor with a list of discrepancies between this ms. and the published score.

K Printed score, corrected and signed by Debussy on July 3, 1895; now in the Sibley Library, Eastman School of Music, Rochester.

R Printed score with Debussy's further corrections and supplementary marks penciled in about 1908; now in the Library of François Lang, Royaumont. M. Henry Goüin, president of the Fondation Royaumont provided the present editor with a complete microfilm of this copy.

S Orchestral parts published by Jobert; copy in the collection of the Cornell University Orchestra.

T Manuscript of Debussy's arrangement for two pianos, with same history as source J.

U Printed score of the two-piano arrangement, published by Jobert; copy in the Cornell University Library.

V Sketch of the whole composition with almost complete indications of orchestration, given by Debussy to Gaby Dupont in 1899; now in the collection of the Robert Owen Lehman Foundation, New York, and published in facsimile by the foundation in 1963.

W Miniature score photographically reproduced from the Jobert full score and published by E. F. Kalmus, New York, 1932.

X Miniature score (newly autographed), Edition Eulenburg No. 1116, Ernst Eulenberg, Ltd., London, Zürich, n.d.

The following notes show all variations among these sources. Where the present edition adopts a reading from one of them that is not common to all, the note is in roman type. Where the present edition does not adopt an interesting variant, the note is in italics. (Various indications of solos and doublings of the winds have been tacitly clarified on the basis of the parts.)

passim	All metronome marks (R)
1–7	Hp.: Debussy's mistake, discussed below (p. 86), is corrected here; all previous editions call for A♭ in addition to the seven notes given here
3	*Fl.: breath mark added after e^2 (R)*
4	Hn. I: tenuto marks (J)
5, 8, 9	*Hn. III: wedges indicating swell are cancelled, and replaced by diminuendo wedges (R); see p. 87 below*
7	Hn. I: tenuto marks and slur (J)
9	Hns. I & III: *più p* (R)
11	D.B.: "A2" might better read "Deux I^{res} Cbs." (cf. m. 93, Vns. I) or "la moitie," since the mark at m. 18, "Unies," implies that from m. 11 on some have been silent.
14	*Vn. II, lower half: e♯^{1} continues throughout the measure, as in the bass (J). Its omission may be a misprint, but possibly Debussy cut out this note on the third beat to allow the horn to be heard more clearly*
15	Vcl.: last note lacks a dot in most previous editions
17	D.B.: last rest is a quarter in previous editions except Eulenburg—obviously a mistake
18	Vn. I: initial *p* (S)
	Vn. II, lower half: last note is c𝄪, in previous editions (including Eulenburg); Mme. Jobert regards this as a mistake for b, which would conform with m. 19
19	All parts: *f* repeated on second and third beats (R)
20	*Bn.: quarter note (J); if this was ever Debussy's intention, he may have changed his mind about it*
22	*Fl. I: even eighths for the last two notes (R, K)*
26	Hn. II: the scores indicate that both Hns. II and IV play B_1; in S, the part for Hns. I and II ignores it
27	Fl. I: ♯ on 12th note (R); the corresponding omission in Fl. II (on its 8th note) still escaped notice, though probably no flutist has ever failed to play as corrected here
28	*Fls.: a slur might be added over the last two eighths, to conform with the second beat, but perhaps Debussy wanted a subtle detaching*
	Bn.: dynamics (R)
29–31	"Cédez . . . au mvt." (R)

31, 34	Hp.: dynamics (R)
32	Tempo warning (R). *R's changed marking of the string chord, from sfz to p, is not adopted here; the danger of an excessive accent has faded as the piece has become more familiar*
40	Vn. I & II: a slur is added here on the second beat to match the first beat and other later versions of the motif. *Many variant slurs in the parts have been ignored*
44	Fl. II & III: accents (R)
	Cl., Bn.: slurs on first two beats (R)
	Hns.: dynamics and rhythms (replacing earlier quarter notes and quarter rests) (R)
	Va.: *mf* and tenutos (R)
50	Bn.: diminuendo (R)
	Hp.: *en dehors* and tenutos (R)
	D.B.: e♭ *an octave lower on the third beat (J)*
52	Hn. II: rest on the third beat, as in Hn. III (S); previous editions had a dotted half, as in Bns.
53	Cl. I: a tie joining the first two A♭s is found in previous editions and might possibly be intentional, though it is contradicted by T and U as well as by all parallel passages
54	Tempo marking (R)
55–58	Winds: slur over all four measures, in each melody part (R); *there are similar slurs over mm. 63–64, 65–66, 67–68, 69–70*
56	Vns., Vas.: dots (S)
57	Winds: accents (R)
58	Vn. II, Va.: Staccato dots might be added as in m. 56, but perhaps Debussy wants a lesser articulation here. Mm. 59–60 show further inconsistencies that seem more probably accidental than significant, but a literal reading of what all the sources agree on will create no disturbance.
60	Vn. I: *p* (S)
62	Hn. II: slur over second beat (S)
	All parts: dynamics (R)
63	Tempo marking (R)
64–65	Vns., Va., Vc.: portamento lines (R)
67	Tempo marking (R)
	Hp. II, lower staff: the eighth note (S) replaces the quarter of earlier scores

69	Hp. II, lower staff: treble clef (S); the bass clef of earlier scores is an obvious engraver's error
70	Hns. II & III: diminuendo wedges (S)
72	*Hp. I: dynamic is* mf *rather than* f *(S)*
73	Tempo marking (R)
83	Hns.: breath mark (R)
	Va.: lower note, e (J, S) is omitted in previous scores
86–92	Hp. II; an impossible B♭ is deleted here
90	Hns.: A breath at the end of the measure, as in m. 83, is probably taken for granted without any mark.
91	Bn. I: *Pierre Boulez reports that in J the first note is B rather than the A♯ that has always offended his ear, but until I can examine the manuscript myself, I rather like the A♯.*
92	Vc., D.B.: tenuto and diminuendo (R). *The cello note D is moved up an octave in R, but this change cannot be evaluated without testing the live sound by ear*
93	Vn. I: staccato dots (S)
	E.H.: *p* (R)
	Hn. I: *p* and diminuendo (R). *In R, "bouché" and "naturel" are crossed out and replaced by "+" whose application to particular notes is uncertain*
96	Vc. solo: crescendo signs (S)
98–99	*Vn. solos: e² and e³ are sustained through these measures (J)*
99	Ob.: diminuendo (R)
99–100	*Ob.: continues to double Fl. II (J); the rest is a nice refinement*
100	Vcl. solo: verbal instruction (R). A crescendo wedge as in the flute part would seem plausible, but perhaps Debussy feared too much crescendo from the cellist—"un peu en dehors" is just enough.
100, 101	Hp., Va.: wedges (R)
	Vn. solos: diminuendos and second *pp* (R)
	Vcl. solo: verbal instruction and crescendo (R)
101	Vcl. solo: crescendo (R)
102	Ob.: diminuendo and second *pp* (R, S)
	Bn. I: tie omitted in most previous scores; an obvious engraver's error
103	Vn. solos: mutes (R)
	"*A tempo*" *marking deleted in R*

105   Vns., Vas.: *pp* between wedges (R); presumably Debussy wants a sudden drop of loudness in the middle of the measure
Vcl. II, D.B.: wedges (R)

Analysis

Unless specified otherwise, all numbered footnotes in the following essays are those of the author. References in the essays to notebooks, letters, and other essays reprinted in the Norton Critical Score have been bracketed and changed to refer to this edition.

Toward an Analytical Appreciation

Every part of this music clings to every other part so firmly, so naturally, that it is hard to identify parts when we want to talk about them. No part torn out of context makes sense. No part spontaneously breaks loose to lodge in our memories as a tune. While we listen, the parts seem to overlap each other, so that the continuity of the whole work is extraordinarily smooth, and our recollection of it at the end is imprecise, though intense. We recognize similarities among many elusive parts, but unless we focus on very small parts we find no exact repetition and no conventional variation of whole phrases or motivic development of balancing phrases. At the end we know we have heard multiple versions of one principal melodic idea, but we suspect we may have missed the clearest statement of that idea. We recall the very beginning: should we call it an introduction? and if so, where does the main action begin? We know that somewhere in the middle of the piece the principal idea was either replaced by another one or vastly transformed, so that toward the end we could welcome its return in shapes nearly like those it had taken long before; but if we try, as many students of the piece have tried, to define three main divisions—beginning, middle, and end, or ABA'—we are likely to disagree with each other and fall into misunderstandings. In all this, incidentally, the music resembles the poem.

There are five points of articulation in the *Prelude* that may well be considered with an open mind before anyone argues about their relative importance. These points are at mm. 30–31, 37, 55, 79, and 94.

Measure 30 is a resting point, the end of a phrase or section, and m. 31 is a somewhat fresh beginning. The note B in melody and bass satisfies the melodic and harmonic motion just before; this B is sustained, diminuendo, so that the sense of cadence—of a goal attained—is clearer here than anywhere else in the piece. Yet the new phrase begins in the clarinet on the upbeat to m. 31, with no complete silence between. And this new phrase, for all its freshness of sound and of accompanying rhythm, is a continuation of earlier melodic ideas rather than a complete contrast, so that many listeners have not been impressed enough to remember this articulation by the time they reached the end of the *Prelude*.

Measure 37 introduces a contrast of melody, of tempo, and of timbre, which is enough to propel the music forward in its longest crescendo and accelerando. The novelty here is greater than that of m. 31. Yet the continuity of sound and rhythm is unbroken at m. 37, so that here, too, many listeners pass by without noting the point as a structural joint.

Measure 55 brings a still more definite contrast of melody, whose beginning overlaps a clear chordal cadence. The two preceding measures are a smooth transition to the new sustained singing of winds in unison, with the new throbbing accompaniment in the strings. There is a sense of being settled in a new key here, D♭, though the major triad is to last only a measure before a new ambiguous chord appears, to remind us, perhaps, of earlier ambiguities. So before the new phrase of melody has finished, to lead into its varied repetition at m. 63, a motif has returned from m. 28, to prove that there is still nothing entirely new.

Measure 79 follows a long, drawn-out cadence and transition on D♭ with a surprising change of harmony to E major (F♭ major?) and a return of the solo flute sound that began the *Prelude*. The flute's melody is recognizably similar to the one it previously played, but different too. The rhythm is different from anything that has gone before. And the way the ideas lead on from this point is different from any earlier section.

At m. 94, the melody and rhythm resemble more closely what we have heard before, at m. 21. And here more than anywhere earlier the key of E is established, the key that will prove eventually, at m. 106, to be the true resting point of the *Prelude*.

Having considered all five points of articulation, we may reasonably debate: if the *Prelude* has a sort of ABA′ structure, does B begin at m. 31, 37, or 55? Does A′ begin at m. 79 or 94?

The midpoint (m. 55) seems to many listeners to be the most important point of articulation, for here begins the melody that makes the strongest contrast with the opening and closing melody. For convenience in naming it, let us note that this midpoint melody is like Chopin's Nocturne in D♭ major, Op. 27, No. 2:

The first half of the *Prelude*, to m. 55, includes a graceful arch of loudness and tempo, rounding off with a tenuous passage in a mood not very different from the beginning, but arousing, by means of melody and harmony, a keen anticipation of the second half. The second half rises to a climax of full loud tone, fades back to the fundamental mood, interrupts this twice with brief bits of animation, and then sinks gradually to a perfect conclusion. To play the second half without the first is to miss much of its effect; to end with the first is almost impossible. The main advantage of talking about the two halves is that we remember their complementary functions. A three-part division always risks suggesting that one of the parts could conceivably stand alone, as the typical minuet without its trio and *da capo* repetition, or as the trio without the minuet. Again, when we talk of two halves, there is no ambiguity about the approximately equal length of the two, whereas any one of three parts may be twice as long as another, so that to talk clearly about three parts in the *Faun* requires that we specify carefully where the second and third parts begin, as in a sonata-form movement, with its exposition, development, and recapitulation. In few sonata-form movements are these divisions as debatable as they are in Debussy's *Prelude*.

The second half of the piece falls into two subdivisions, more strongly contrasted with each other than are any subdivisions within the first half. Measure 79 uniquely corresponds to the division at the midpoint. Thus, it is possible to think of three main parts of the piece as ABA′, with B and A′ together balancing the long, complex A.

But for some listeners the division in the middle (m. 55) is subordinate to both m. 79 and m. 37. Thus Denijs Dille, in a long discussion of the formal novelty of the *Prelude*,[1] labels his main sections as follows:

m. 1   A
    37   B I
    55   B II
    79   A'

Other listeners find the chief subdivision of the first half at m. 31. This is the view of Jean Barraqué, for instance.[2] He strengthens his case by pointing to a resemblance between the second part within his A and the first of his A', which leads to what he recognizes as a genuine recapitulation only at m. 94. Barraqué correctly states that these mobile sections (mm. 31–36 and 76–93) make the piece as a whole somewhat resemble a sonata form, while the exposition, contrasting middle part, and recapitulation make it resemble a "song form," like that of many classical dances with trios. At least one listener, Ernst Decsey, begins a twofold middle section at m. 31.[3] Decsey then finds subdivisions of every part to match the "bar form," AA'B, and further subdivisions of these B's into aa'b.

All these different analyses are plausible. Need we prefer one to another? The experts' disagreement can be left unreconciled, and can be used by any patient student simply to learn the music. Perhaps the disagreement is more about the meaning of the labels than about the way the music coheres. Or perhaps the music coheres in more than one way; that is, different ways of organizing the experience of listening to it are complementary, not contradictory. As we shall observe again and again with respect to details within the whole form, Debussy's music characteristically evades or blurs all sorts of classifications and abstractions. It is unique. Yet it is not blurry itself, but supple, precise, clearly articulated, and balanced. It may even be called, in some sense, logical. Its unique logic becomes more compelling to the ear as we consider alternative analyses. Its whole shape sticks in our minds finally, and we may discard labels or readily understand anyone else's brand new ones if they fit the piece at all.

    1. Denijs Dille, *Inleiding tot het vormbegrip bij Debussy*, in *Mélanges . . . van den Borren*, Antwerp, 1945, p. 175. For a ms. translation of this article I am indebted to Professor Donald J. Grout.
    2. See below, p. 162. Compare also the anonymous analysis in N. Dufourcq, ed., *Larousse de la musique*, Paris, 1957.
    3. See below, p. 156.

Toward an Analytical Appreciation

A new suggestion is proposed here: that the Chopinesque melody which begins the second half of the piece is not really a new theme, but a culminating expansion of the principal theme rather like the refrain or chorus of an aria or song that releases the flow prepared by a less tuneful stanza. The layout of the main melodic lines in the chart on pp. 76–78 is designed to make this suggestion attractive. Wherever the notes appear at the left margin, they present a variant of the same downward melodic motion. Where notes approach the right margin, they may possibly be related to fragments of the original sinuous curve (mm. 3 and 4).

If this proposal were insisted on, we might call everything up to the last quarter of the piece (m. 79) Section A, and call the remainder B. But let us reject that as too far-fetched. Further, let us admit the "flowing motif" (mm. 24, 28, 68, 73, 96) and the "syncopated motif" (mm. 39, 54, 67) as new material, not obviously derived from the opening phrase. The participation of these motifs in the various parts of the piece, often in the accompaniment as well as the main melody, is enough to mark the extraordinary interlocking of parts. Also, the unobtrusive introduction of such important unifying motifs is peculiar; this peculiarity, more than the resemblance of contours in the opening phrases, makes the full-blown melody of Section B organically one with Section A. Finally, the unique continuity of melody motivates the fluctuations of loudness and speed. To find just the right amount of fluctuation, performers must be continually aware of motivic relations that bind the whole melody together.

The continuity depends not only on melodic motifs, but also, of course, on chords and their progressions, and on the relationships among pitches in both chords and melodies. If we think of the rise and fall of melodies as co-ordinating the dimension of pitch with that of time, then the harmonic aspect of the music is a third dimension, a deep background from which the melody can come toward us and into which chords can open vistas. In some kinds of music, melody and its accompanying harmony can be distinguished as "elements." Saint-Saëns, for one, made much of this distinction. To him and some other listeners Debussy's *Prelude* seemed deficient in melody, while the euphonious chords and unconventional successions of chords seemed to hold attention for their own sake, regardless of their place in the long time span. But in fact the thrilling quality of the chords depends on their whole moving context, and especially on their relationship to melody, while at

hypothetical simplification

flowing motif

whole-tone scale

syncopated motif

Toward an Analytical Appreciation

William W. Austin

Toward an Analytical Appreciation 79

the same time every note in a melodic line has harmonic value too—often more than one value in equivocal balance. Debussy's lifelong friend Paul Dukas understood this relation of melody and harmony at once. Debussy himself, in 1893, spoke of "melodic harmonies" in Palestrina.[4] Later he claimed for himself the right to "blend the elements."[5] Often he insisted on the primacy of melody in his own music, and on whole contexts as determining the value of chords. Perhaps his way of beginning the *Faun,* like his earlier orchestral suite *Printemps,* with unaccompanied melody is a clue to his kind of harmony. In any case, we do well to consider the harmonic aspect of the melody before we focus on chords.

In the opening phrase of melody the first and last notes are especially memorable. Neither of them sounds like a tonic, a suitable resting point, but they are not clearly subordinated to the note that ultimately proves to be the tonic, E, or to any other note. They do not point ahead. They hang in our memories uncertainly. They seem to vibrate with uncertainty. This uncertainty is not at all the same as mere harmonic indifference, such as characterizes speech melody or some electronic music. Debussy's notes are in precise relations to each other, ambiguous relations that suggest more than they make clear or emphatic. Our memories of these notes surely work throughout the composition, accumulating as the various harmonic possibilities of the notes become explicit in accompanying chords and melodic contexts.

The first note, C♯, returns again and again with a new chord almost every time. First it is the dissonant major seventh against a D-major triad (m. 11); then, transferred to the end of the phrase, it is a chord-root in a context that makes it sound like a dominant (at the end of m. 17). Both these meanings of the C♯ intensify its appeal for melodic motion. In each case the melody is frustrated; the motion does not satisfy the appeal. But now our note returns and lasts a long time as an added sixth against the E-major triad (m. 21). The melody resolves the note into that triad, so that we feel that here, if anywhere, is its fundamental, normal meaning. Yet the melody does not pause. Next, our C♯ makes a most poignant dissonance against the dominant-ninth chord on E (m. 26), and the melody flows forward to the cadence on B (m. 30), re-

---

4. Debussy, in a letter to Poniatowski, as quoted in Lockspeiser, *Debussy: His Life and Mind,* I, 172.

5. Robert de Flers, in an interview with Debussy in *Figaro,* as quoted by Vallas, *Debussy,* 1958, p. 242.

solving our first note at last, so that we can take a calm breath in preparation for further developments.

We may lose track of the C♯ in the course of the piece, though perhaps we feel its identity without consciously recognizing it when it appears in various guises, particularly as ninth in the dominant chord (m. 37), then respelled as minor third (m. 46), and finally as temporary tonic (m. 56 ff). We recognize it when it begins the main melody once more (m. 94), accompanied again by the dominant-ninth chord on E. This time it pulls that chord to its normal resolution on A, the subdominant, where C♯ sounds sweetest as major third. The melody lingers and meanders over this "Amen" chord, but instead of letting things proceed to a final tonic chord, the melody leads back to the C♯ with a magical new accompaniment, its own seventh chord (m. 100). Only now does the melody lead smoothly down a scale to resolve this first note, and all the accompanying voices too, in a fully satisfactory tonic chord. What remains is coda. Here the C♯ is part of the chord based on the last note from the first phrase (m. 107), a chord that epitomizes the piece, and glides calmly into the tonic, with which it shares its two remaining notes all the while.

A similar account of what happens to the last note from the first phrase, A♯, reveals another strand of unity in the piece. This note, appearing for the first time and surprising us in itself, is made iridescent by the two surprising chords that accompany it while it lasts. Both chords could arise out of the A♯ as root, or the first chord might be a nonharmonic preparation for the second; the two suggest that the note is either the second degree of a G♯-minor scale, or else a dominant in E♭ (D♯) major. But these suggestions are so incongruous with the preceding melody that most listeners reject them and submit to the chords as sheer sound or color or synesthetic thrill. The silence, the repetition of the chords, and the tenuousness of any melodic transition from our last note of melody to the next phrase—all these extraordinary things make the note and its chords extremely prominent. Still, these things work as they do only because of the preceding melody. If the piece were to begin with the A♯ of m. 4, all the rich color of the chords would seem banal. So, when the A♯ and its seventh chord return (mm. 14, 17) they no longer keep the melody in suspense, but rather move it forward. When the A♯ returns again with a new seventh chord (m. 28), it is a melodic high point, fulfilling the chief function in the traditional major scale, leading-tone to the cadential B.

In the second half of the piece A♯ (=B♭) is prominent as high note of the broad "chorus" (m. 57). Here it assumes the added-sixth function that was earlier associated with the first note, the C♯. In the last moments of Section B the solo violin lingers on the high note, while the chord intensifies its pull with a seventh (mm. 77–78). Toward the end of the piece, A♯ with its dominant chord modifies the C♯ with its dominant (m. 100), and then, as the melody moves, our note (B♭) works the great twist of harmony (m. 103) that leads into the final cadence. Here it is transformed from a sharpened fourth degree to a flattened fifth (counting up from E), and the accompanying chord makes it a dominant seventh. As the note resolves downward, the chord of resolution is not the expected F, but better than that—F♯ minor, from which conventional logic can proceed through the dominant to the firm tonic. In this light the fantastic suggestions of the very first chords acquire more meaning than we could have recognized before. Finally, in the coda an accompanying voice recalls A♯, and in its very last appearance a countermelody moves from it through the first note to the tonic, summing up the piece without emphasis, leaving us with both the important notes vivid though calm. The chord that appeared first in the piece has returned at the very end, to lead back to the melody.

One more note deserves special notice: the lowest note of the first phrase, which opposes the first note with an inherently ambiguous interval. Debussy always spells this note G, so that it counts as augmented fourth below the opening C♯, but it sounds also like F𝄪, making a diminished fifth, pushing toward the G♯ that belongs to the major scale and the major tonic chord. This low note works most definitely as F𝄪 when it appears in the recapitulation preparing the G♯ that is to replace it altogether in the last versions of the melody (mm. 99–100). Then as the melody moves on, it touches a high G instead of the expected G♯, and this G pulls definitely down through F♯ to the big cadence on E. The ambiguity—F𝄪 or G—is fully exploited and resolved in this last long phrase. Prior to this, however, the melody has sometimes shed this ambiguity (mm. 23, 79, 86), and, more important, the ambiguity has been otherwise exploited, without resolution, at critical points in the piece. Thus the questionable low note and the first note are heard together in melody and bass (m. 31) to provoke a whole phrase of ambiguous harmony. As the melody dissolves in preparation for the chorus (m. 51), there is a marvelous rising passage in which our low note is transformed into high note and then into first note of a variant of the theme (m. 52). And, most important of all, the two notes, alternating, provide the bass for the "chorus" (m. 55). The low G here seems like some spongy ground underfoot; where we would have expected to move to a firm dominant or subdominant, we find instead this unfamiliar, soft harmony that complements the tonic in a new way; we shudder even as we step on, back to the tonic.

The low note (G) and the first note (C♯) in co-ordination at the points just discussed suggest a whole-tone scale. This suggestion is elaborated briefly, first as an ornamental flurry in the melody (mm. 32–33 and 35–36) and then as a single pulsing chord (mm. 64, 66). In neither case does the whole-tone scale last through a phrase. And nowhere else in the piece does Debussy resort to this scale. It is an incidental phenomenon, subordinate to the progress of the melody, and supporting that progress at just the right stages. Except for the fact that in some other pieces Debussy used the whole-tone scale more extensively and conspicuously, its discreet uses here might go unnoticed. But they are worth noticing for the sake of their connection with the prominent notes in the first phrase, whose ambiguous relation they exaggerate.

The susceptibility of the C♯ and the G and their connecting line of melody to being harmonized with various chordal accompaniments (mm. 11, 21, 26, and, with the low note adjusted, m. 100) is the outstanding harmonic feature of the *Prelude*. Listeners who have advanced beyond a first acquaintance with the piece marvel at this feature, often without much concern for the latter half of the opening phrase, the supplementary motifs, the chorus melody, or any account of the form as a whole. If such listeners proceed to generalize about Debussy's harmony and its revolutionary significance for the history of styles, they go astray, separating melody and harmony even more crudely than Saint-Saëns ever did, whereas Debussy's actual procedure, as examined here, unites melody and harmony more subtly and firmly. Debussy does not simply show off a bit of melody against various surprising chords. Rather he uses the chords to support the onward movement of the melody. He chooses freely among many harmonic possibilities, but he chooses each time with the purpose of fitting the moment into its place in a long, continuous whole. His choices cannot be explained by any rule. But their rightness is felt by anyone who persists in following the whole piece as we have done.

The rightness of the chords in their places can be shown still more clearly, if still not explained, by detaching the bass part and surveying its whole length (see the example on p. 83). Where two notes appear lined up vertically in the example, the upper one is the sounding bass and

Toward an Analytical Appreciation

Brackets show strong progressions by a fifth down or a fourth up.

the lower one the "fundamental bass" or harmonic root. This survey of the basses shows the hierarchy of pitch relations that makes the final cadence as satisfying as that of more conventionally organized pieces. Moreover, this survey shows how harmonic movement contributes a rhythmic element to the form: in the first half of the piece the motion is very irregular, often slow but occasionally fast; in Section B, the motion is regular until it subsides at the end of the section; in Section A' there is irregular motion again, but not as irregular as at first.

The chords above the bass are predominantly richer than triads—seventh chords and ninth chords, as we have observed in connection with the C♯. Pure major triads in root position occur only for the two chief cadences (mm. 30 and 106) and for the chorus melody (mm. 55, 57, 63, 65, 67, 69). Minor chords are even rarer, and each of them is as potent as a dissonance (mm. 25, 59, 61, 95, 96, 104). The richer chords, on the contrary, have no harshness and scarcely any tension. Their dissonance —in the traditional technical sense of the term—is accepted and relished quietly without any connotation of urgency or climax such as these chords usually carried in earlier music. Yet it is the relation of the rich chords to the purely consonant chords and the relation of both to melody that gives the richness its new meaning.

At two points Debussy openly violates the old rules that forbade parallel motion of either dissonant intervals or pure fifths and octaves. Seventh chords succeed each other just before the end of the first half (mm. 48–49). Prominent fifths occur between flute and English horn near the very end of the piece (m. 102). No one today hears these parallels as incorrect, because similar effects are common in much later music. Indeed, since Debussy showed that such things could be beautiful, they have become innocuous and often banal. But his imitators rarely find such contexts for them as he found. In his contexts, the parallels that he wrote have not come to sound banal. Perhaps it is even possible to feel something of the dizziness that his parallels must have caused sympathetic listeners when the piece was new. At least it is possible to appreciate Debussy's discretion in saving the device for only two places, which make a kind of balance and so contribute to the continuity of the whole piece.

Many of the chord progressions, on the other hand, are orthodox. Parallel motion is no substitute for older procedures, but an additional resource combined with them in a new and comprehensive logic.

Among the chord progressions a fair number could easily be assigned Roman numerals for diatonic scale degrees in accordance with traditional academic theory of harmony. Not quite so easily, by stretching this theory to its farthest chromatic elaborations, all the chords except the parallel ones could be accounted for. But in every phrase there are novel, questionable progressions along with the strong traditional ones, and the sense of chromatic freedom is so pervasive that the effort to label every chord seems out of proportion with any resulting insight. The mere survey of roots on the staff serves our purpose more efficiently than a strained traditional numbering.

Our survey evades the questions of tonality and modulation, which traditional number-analysis would require us to answer. Evasion of these questions is perhaps the most appropriate tactic. We recall Debussy's letter to Gauthier-Villars playfully disclaiming "reverence for the key" and asserting instead the demonstrability of "a mode that tries to contain all the nuances." Debussy made similar assertions on other occasions, both earlier and later in his life. He never divulged the "logical demonstration" that his comprehensive "mode" would need if it were to be taught to young composers, as the traditional major-minor system is still taught. Twentieth-century theorists and teachers have wrestled with the question of tonality in new music, and several have claimed to supply a "logical demonstration," but they disagree with each other. Some have appealed to history for an understanding of Debussy's attenuated tonality as a stage in the development toward Schoenberg's alleged "atonality," while others have prophesied that Debussy's comprehensive logic, rightly systematized, would prove Schoenberg's departure a mistake or at most an alternative development rather than the inevitable or best possible end of an historical process. Prudent historians give no comfort to either of these partisan views. A wise analysis, then, until the course of history necessitates a better one, evades the decision about tonality in many of the chord progressions. We can say that the piece ends after all in E major and that Section B begins and ends in D♭, while we prefer to wonder rather than decide whether the beginning is in E, or C♯, or some other key, or none at all. Wonderment is surely an appropriate response to this music, which analysis should serve not to allay but to intensify.

The wonderful uncertainties and the elusive logic of Debussy's harmony are effective even in a piano arrangement. They are immensely intensified by his choices of instrumental colors. Furthermore, the colors make some independent contribution to the whole form. Thus the basic sound of the piece at beginning and end, modified of course by many fluctuations, is that of the flute solo accompanied by harp and muted string orchestra. When the harmony arrives at its chief cadences (mm. 30, 51, 74, 106), the strings give them a gratifying fullness. Then a sharp contrast of more penetrating sound introduces the next phrase in each case, with horns or clarinet (or both) leading off into strange harmonic byways. At each of these articulating points the harp is also present, with a different role in each case, yet similar too, involving single notes like punctuation marks rather than chords. The two occurrences of harmonics for the harp (mm. 50–51 and 108–09) are especially neat, telling, and well-balanced. The harp first plays its traditionally favorite full sound of continuous broken chords to set motion under way for the expository phrases (mm. 21–30), then to assist in building the climax (mm. 63–70), and finally to ripple calmly in pure consonance when the flute resumes the melody (mm. 79–90). Above all, the harp exploits its glissando to give a shudder to two of the most surprising chords (mm. 4 and 7, 90 and 91), where the sense of tonality is most baffled.

The harp glissando merits an extended discussion.[6] Gliding over all the strings of a diatonic scale was a special effect well used by Berlioz, the first composer to make the harp a normal part of his orchestra. Players found it shamefully easy. Using the pedal mechanism to tune the whole harp to a four-note chord and playing this in the same easy way was an invention attributed to the harpist Elias Parish-Alvars (1808–49), from whom Liszt borrowed it to ornament diminished-seventh chords in his *Mephisto Waltz* and *Dante Symphony*. Debussy, and after him Ravel, gave the effect so many appropriate uses that it became a normal part of harp music. Some of their successors used it so glibly that it was soon used up. The opening chord of the *Faun* is doubtless the one most famous and influential example of the glissando, and one of the best-remembered sounds of the piece. The glissando on a different chord toward the end, with a pause between its up-sweep and down-sweep, is equally admirable though not so often noted. And the formal balance provided by the four measures in the context of the whole piece is the most admirable aspect of all.

Such a prominent sound might be thought to have belonged to Debussy's first inspiration for the *Prelude*. But in his piano reduction there is no trace of it. Could he possibly have added this memorable touch during rehearsals? In his orchestral sketch, undated, the glissando

---

6. See Marcel Tournier, *La Harpe*, Paris, 1959.

appears at the beginning but not at the later, balancing point. Could he have added in rehearsals only this exquisitely calculated balance?

Such a conspicuous effect as the glissando might seem to call for special pains in notation and proofreading. But there are anomalies here! The instructions for the pedals in the score cannot be followed literally. They call for a nonexistent eighth string in the octave, or else for one string to be in two positions (A in mm. 4–7, B in mm. 90–91). The harpist's part shows this mistake corrected once, left standing the other time. (There are, in fact, as shown in the score, two harp parts; the first player has the first glissando and the second the other. But it is not difficult for one harpist to play both parts, omitting only a few variant doublings in the tutti, mm. 67–70.) Debussy's intention is not in doubt. The player can realize it as he pleases, and smile to himself about the composer's absentmindedness.

The horn parts show the union of melody and harmony in a special way. As important as these parts are, they are subordinate to the main melody until the very end, where they give the melody a final echo, as from a far distance, fantastically combining with the shadowy sound of the violins' low string. At the beginning, more typically, a horn enters just after the first chord. Its entrance has an accent to make it distinct even though the note belongs to the chord. Then the horn moves to the second chord, and over this chord a second horn completes the countermelody, which is a free imitation of the flute's curve:

The continuity of the line shared by the horns must be recognized by the players if it is to have its effect on listeners. The effect can be spoiled if the player of the notes C and D makes too much of his swell. When Debussy conducted, he replaced the swell by a diminuendo. But the best performance of these notes will be affected not only by the reminiscence of the beginning, but also by an anticipation of what is yet to come, swelling indeed:

Flute, Horn, m. 13

When the flute returns to this curve (m. 13), a horn rises unobtrusively out of the accompanying chords with a tiny motif from the former second-horn part; it is joined again by its mate to push the phrase onward, until all four horns can support the melody in its impassioned gaspings (m. 19). The correspondence of these two passages (mm. 3–5 and m. 13) is even more remarkable than the subtle effectiveness of each one alone.

Horn notes, very deep and soft, help to bind together the expository phrase (mm. 21–30) and the recapitulation (mm. 94–100). A metallic accent by the muted horns propels the change of mood after the first cadence (m. 31), and this is balanced in Section A' by the muted slow trill (mm. 83–84 and 90–91), the slow staccato chords (m. 85), an isolated stifled accent (m. 92), a hand-stopped note and a final fading into open tone (mm. 93–94). But the mutes return at the end.

Throughout most of the "chorus," Section B, horns blend into the full orchestral sound. With the other woodwinds accompanying the strings (mm. 63–70), they give a panting urgency to the climax that reminds Lockspeiser of the similar accompanying figure for horns in Tchaikovsky's Fantasy-Overture, *Romeo and Juliet*.[7] But Debussy's use of this effect is brief and unemphatic, provided that the strings' melody is kept well in the foreground as his dynamic marks indicate. More prominently, the horns frame this section with brief statements of the syncopated motif (mm. 47, 74) rising from and blending back into the chordal background.

There are special coloristic devices in the string accompaniments that also serve the form. A tremolo begins with the bows over the fingerboard (m. 11) for an extraordinarily soft rustling; it rises to a mild forte and breaks off on a dissonant chord. In the recapitulation (m. 94), there is a still softer trembling of the fingers, while again the bows are drawn slowly over the fingerboard; this time the effect continues, with little rises and falls, until it fades away on the magical seventh chord of the C♯ (m. 100). This latter passage, in addition, has unmuted solo violins and

---

7. Lockspeiser, *op. cit.*, I, 51.

cello in octaves, recalling the one solo violin that played a codetta to the "chorus" (mm. 75–78). As the solo cello goes on beyond this section, delicately mirroring the flute solo, perhaps it is not too farfetched to think that it balances the one prominent bit for the cello section, a sardonic murmur beginning with *spiccato* repeated notes (mm. 31, 34). If this connection is allowed, then the last full phrase represents a sort of reconciliation and fulfillment of every preceding phrase in the piece.

The last phrases have a further blending of color and harmony in the soft tinklings of the antique cymbals. Debussy's use of these instruments, first introduced by Berlioz in his *Romeo and Juliet,* is their chief single reason for existence in many a percussion player's battery. When an orchestra lacks them, their notes can be played on the glockenspiel, but the cymbals are better, their shimmer around the pitches matching the gentle way in which the tonic is finally confirmed.

The woodwind choir, made up of three flutes, two oboes and English horn, two clarinets, and two bassoons, works as a whole less often than it provides soloists, but its occasional functioning as a choir is not negligible. Lockspeiser has pointed out [8] how Debussy's sketch assigned to the strings some sounds that he later gave to the winds, greatly enhancing the effect: the first chord (m. 4) and the first statement of the "chorus" melody (mm. 55–61). There is one other spot where this occurs: the first time that the melody rises to the high octave of the first note (mm. 45–47). These three appearances of the wind choir guarantee that its use, along with the horns, to accompany the strings' "chorus" at the climax (mm. 63–70), will not seem excessive.

In several of these passages the conductor Donald Rauscher has pointed out problems of balance.[9] Rauscher's severest criticism is directed at the finicky doubling in the transitional passage that leads to the "chorus" (mm. 53–54):

> Debussy unfortunately gives the show away in measures 53 and 54. His apparent attempt to portray the dappled light and shadow of the Faun's idyllic environment results in an irritating sense of out-of-tuneness in the woodwinds. The first oboe joins the clarinet solo at the unison, and the second flute (no doubt representing the sunlit spots) plays every other tone, also at the unison. This is tone-painting carried to the extreme—the extreme at which the theory exceeds the limits of practicality.[10]

8. Lockspeiser, *Debussy . . . facsimile,* in *Music and Letters,* XLV (1964), 301.
9. Donald J. Rauscher, *Orchestration, Scores, & Scoring,* New York, 1963, p. 214 ff.
10. *Ibid.,* p. 218.

Undoubtedly this passage demands of the players the kind of concern characteristic of chamber music, rather than the orchestral player's usual reliance on the conductor, or the would-be concerto soloist's self-indulgent expressivity. If the players are up to the demands, the writing is not impractical. As for its pictorial associations, they are as dubious here as they are throughout the piece. Surely Debussy is asking for very special sounds, not merely carrying out for the score-reader's amusement some literary theory. The special sounds are typical of his adventurous imagination, and such unusual demands on the players are especially typical of his later music.

It may be helpful, once again, to consider this difficult passage in relation to the whole form: it is the third of four turning-points at which the clarinet takes the lead. The first of these is very easy, brief, and beautiful (m. 20), with the clarinet unaccompanied, free to make its utmost diminuendo and to adjust its ritard accordingly. The next is deliberately a bit shocking—a loud and sustained tone at the top of the instrument's "throat" register, such as textbooks warn composers to use only with caution (m. 31); its color is just right for this spot. The last is at the end of Section B, accompanying the solo violin (mm. 75–76); here the clarinet's sweetest tone has its consoling effect. If the clarinet player thinks about all four passages together, and if the flutist and oboist really listen to him before they join him (mm. 51–53), their difficult "dappled" effect can come off.

One detail originally imagined for clarinet, as indicated in the sketch, was transferred to the bassoon, which not only makes a clearer contrast to the flutes and strings that it accompanies here (m. 28), but also allows the clarinet solo just afterward to make its contrast more telling. A further refinement of the same detail, made later than the piano reduction, is the shortening of the first trill by the value of an eighth note, so that the second trill, lasting longer, is more expressive. The last refinement, crescendo on the first trill and diminuendo on the second, was introduced in the Royaumont score.

Finally we turn to the flute part. The *Faun* changed the very character of the flute as orchestral instrument. From music of the eighteenth and nineteenth centuries we can still think of the flute as a fife, a whistle, a fluttery and birdlike personage, or perhaps as a disembodied, if blessed, spirit. But from Debussy and his successors we know it also as sultry, smouldering with pagan dreams. Wagner had tended to neglect the flute; for the faun's reed he would naturally have chosen the oboe or

English horn. But French players, particularly Claude-Paul Taffanel (1844–1908), had developed a new, relaxed, expressive technique of playing, and Debussy gave them the best showpiece in their whole repertory. The first note of the piece, to which the flute returns so often and which it sustains so long, is, according to Rauscher, "probably the most flexible tone on the instrument," and Debussy's context "gives the performer the opportunity to color it as he will." [11] The general range of the whole melody is not that of a coloratura soprano, whose warblings had often inspired the flute, but rather the gentle lyric range, supremely "sweet and expressive."

The flute part has a problem too—when to breathe. Debussy writes as though the player's breath could last indefinitely. But perhaps this problem is not insoluble if the flutist and conductor agree on what Debussy means by a "very moderate" tempo—not quite the "rather slow" of his sketch and his piano reduction—and if the flutist begins the longest phrase, the expository one (m. 21), with the new lightness of tone that Debussy recommends.

Rhythm and tempo in Debussy's music attract less attention than harmony and orchestral sound, but in spite of this it can be argued that Debussy's greatest, most forward-looking achievement was in the realm of rhythm. Just this argument is advanced by Brunello Rondi.[12] He credits Debussy with having discovered the "essence" of twentieth-century rhythm, opening the way for Stravinsky, Prokofiev, Varèse, Messiaen, and all the rest. Rondi describes Debussy's rhythms only vaguely, with little reference to particular pieces. As stimulating as his descriptions are, they no more succeed in explaining the "essence" than the many descriptions of harmony and sound succeed in explaining their quintessence. If we are right about the interactions of harmony and sound with melody, it may well turn out that rhythm, too, depends on melody, and that our understanding of Debussy's rhythm must depend on our relating it to all the other aspects of his music in particular pieces.

The *Faun*'s rhythm is elusive, like its melody, harmony, and sound. We cannot grasp the rhythmic life with our first attempts. Yet when we feel it as a good performer must, we know that it is strong and sure, for all its subtlety. It is like melody and harmony in its strength as well as in its elusiveness.

The rhythmic strength is not a matter of accent or emphasis, but

---

11. *Ibid.*, p. 214.
12. Brunello Rondi, *Prospettiva della musica moderna*, Rome, 1956, p. 13 ff.

rather of continuity. No one is likely to tap his foot with the beats. Yet even a listener who had never heard the music before, never seen a score, never seen a conductor's beats, would feel this continuity, interrupted only by the silence at m. 6. He would feel this continuity embracing the quiet pulsation of rhythm that becomes more or less clear in various passages, and he would assume that all the motion of either melody or accompaniment is related to some obscure, slow, gentle pulse. The more he liked the sounds and the melody, the more he would trust this pulse. If for him, on the contrary, the allure of the sounds and the pull of the melody were not strong enough, he might complain about the rhythm, as Curt Sachs has complained, that it "never gets anywhere," [13] or simply that its slow motion is "depressing." If he loved the melody and listened many times before trying to count out the rhythm, he might make some further superficial observations: that the pulsation first comes to the fore along with the volume of sound (mm. 17-20, 37-44), but that it is not steady until almost the end of Section A (m. 49); that throughout Section B it is steady but still veiled by continual syncopation; that in Section A' it is hardly identifiable. He might wonder at the accelerando in Section A and the several ritards. He would hesitate to characterize the rhythm or tempo as a whole, or to point to any one passage as representing a norm of pulsation for the piece. He might suspect that the very elusiveness of the rhythm serves the extraordinary continuity.

Debussy's verbal indications of the tempo fit our innocent listener's impressions. They are mostly imprecise. In the score as published, they are fairly copious, and it is interesting to see how Debussy amplified and refined these indications at several stages after he had sketched the whole composition. The table on p. 93 facilitates a comparison of five stages.

The most important discrepancy here, though every one is interesting, occurs at the beginning of our Section A' (m. 79): in the piano reduction Debussy indicates that the tempo from Section B is to continue here; in the score, however, he refers back to the beginning of the *Prelude*. Does this mean that his own interpretation changed? Or did he suppose that he had found a better means of suggesting to the performers what he wanted all along? Or can we guess that his concept

---

13. Curt Sachs, *Rhythm and Tempo*, New York, 1952, p. 360.

Sketch	Reduction for two pianos	Measure	MS. score	Published score	Measure	Royaumont additions
Assez lent	Assez lent	1	Très modéré	Très modéré	1	MM $\.=44$
retenu	riten.	20	retenu	retenu [clar. only]	20	cédez
Moins lent		21				au mvt.
					29–30	(sans trainer)
	Dans ce 3/4 les croches	29–30			31	
	gardent le même mouv^t.	31	$\.=\.$	$\.=\.$	32	$\.=72$
	En animant un peu	32				
	Animez toujours	37	En animant	En animant	37	
		44	Toujours en animant	Toujours en animant	44	
		47[–50]	En retenant jusqu'aux			
	Retenu	48–50	4 bémols			
		49–50		retenu	49–50	$\.=60$
	1er mouvement	51	1er mouv^t.	1er mouv^t.	51	cédez un peu
					54	$\.=56$
		55	Même mouv^t. et très soutenu	[same]	55	En animant
					63	Toujours animé
					67	cédez un peu
					73	$\.=60$
	Retenu	75			74	
	Même mouv^t.	79		Mouv^t du Début	79	$\.=84$
				Un peu plus animé	83	
		86	1er mouv^t.	1er mouv^t.	86	
	En retenant			Dans le mouv^t	90	
		92		plus animé		
	Mouv^t du début (avec	93	Dans le 1er mouv^t avec	retenu	93	
	plus de langueur)	94	plus de langueur	[same]	94	
	retenu	102	Retenu	Retenu	102	
	Plus lent	103	(a tempo)	(a tempo) *Oboe part*	103	delete a tempo
				Suivez		
		105		Très retenu	105	
	Très lent	106		Très lent et très retenu	106	
		107		jusqu'à la fin		

of the piece was flexible, and that he would want each team of pianists and each conductor, having considered all the markings, to take none literally but rather to use discretion in making the tempo changes contribute somehow to the unity and shape of the piece? The last possibility seems likely, especially since at the beginning of Section A′ the relation between the faint pulse and the melody is new—hardly closer to the relation at the beginning of the piece than to the relation between the stronger pulse and the different melody in Section B. The metronome markings of the Royaumont score show no exact equivalence; the ♩ at m. 79 is a trifle slower than the ♩. at m. 1, and the conductor's beat divides the new pulse in two. Moreover, a flexible conception of the tempo throughout the piece and a reliance on the performers' tact and taste are normal for composers before Stravinsky. The tempo marks of most music are only suggestions. They cannot resolve our hypothetical innocent listener's wonderings, but in studying them we can marvel more and more at the unity and shape of the piece.

Our innocent listener might suspect that Debussy left his performers even more discretion than he actually did. He might imagine that much of the piece would be written as a cadenza, or a recitative, or with fermatas—all traditional devices for denying the measured pulse and its subdivisions. Some performers, to be sure, *take* liberties with Debussy's rhythm as if he had not measured it at all. But the best performers respect the measure as well as all the tempo marks, and use them to create an effect of true spontaneous freedom, whereas arbitrarily free interpretations, paradoxically, sound contrived.

The best performers, then, must feel the pulse indicated in Debussy's measures as a foil for their moderate freedom of tempo. They feel the pulse even when it is hidden from the innocent listener. They feel it continuously throughout the piece, helping to make a unity through all the amazing diversity of motion and rest, and especially through all the changes of tempo, both striking ones and subtle ones.

In the 110 measures of the piece, five different time signatures are used. Nineteen measures have a change of signature from the preceding measure. Most of these are in Section A, none in B, enough in A′ to counterbalance the fact that the prevailing signature of A′ has not appeared in A or B at all. These simple observations from the score (or from a good conductor's beat) can assist a persevering though nonperforming listener to feel the rhythm.

One more such observation may be useful. In 53 measures there are *gruppetti,* dividing a beat into some motion that is exceptional from the point of view of the time signature. The triplets of the opening melody and the duplets at the last cadence (mm. 105–06) are characteristic of the piece, and of Debussy's rhythm in general. His time signatures do not commit him to a norm of subdividing the beat; he freely alternates subdivisions. This freedom can serve to reinforce the slow pulse. It prevents any subdivision from sounding like a fast pulse, and in a good performance it constitutes another wonderful strand of unity in variety.

Another kind of observation from the score may be relevant to the quality of rhythm in the music: melodies often begin on a downbeat, and they often lift with an upbeat; unlike many melodies of German and Italian composers throughout the period of common practice, Debussy's melodies less often lead from the upbeat into an emphatic downbeat. The distinctiveness of Debussy in this respect is great enough to make some musicians suppose that he no longer thought of upbeats and downbeats, but used all beats as mere weightless measurements, as some later composers have meant to do. But this exaggerates his novelty. The exaggeration probably betrays a neglect of the chord progressions, which, as we have seen, make a distinctive rhythmic pattern, but not an utterly weightless one. The chords move variously, gently, so as to support the melody in its more various motion, and when the melody is ready to rest, the chords move with it, settling down with a traditional cadence.

For Debussy the word "rhythm" denoted no mere durational parameter of tones or groups of tones. It meant quality of movement. In his piano preludes he sometimes asked for a "caressing rhythm," and once he urged "this rhythm should have the sonorous value of a landscape, cold and sorrowful." The rhythms of the *Faun,* likewise, should have values that we might associate with Mallarmé's Sicilian marsh, with his "nostalgia . . . light . . . finesse . . . malaise," and with "the rising movement of the poem."

Indeed, Debussy's music can finally help a reader feel the marvelous "rising movement" in Mallarmé's *Faun,* and the many elusive verbal rhythms that contribute to the poem's sure continuity.

When he referred to the "rising movement" of the poem, perhaps Debussy meant something like this: the faun's flute dominates the first half of the poem, with its secrets and its dream of transforming our thought; then the flute is rejected in favor of speech, which unveils, thrills, and defines our mistakes; but beyond speech, of course, are endless desires and sleep and silence. Debussy's flute solo and its developments in the first half of the *Prelude* correspond to the first half of the poem; his choral melody rivals Mallarmé's and the faun's speech; his final section carries us beyond, to desires and sleep and silence. This interpretation is the conjecture of Professor Hans-Jost Frey, Mallarmé scholar, which he proposed to me after he had read my study up to this point. Professor Frey further suggests a correspondence of leading motifs: the wind is exhaled through the flute (line 18) and drawn up again to heaven (line 22); then the grapes are sucked (line 57) and puffed up again (line 60); the swaying motion of Debussy's main melody, down-up-down-up, seems to Frey to match this poetic idea, and both poetic and musical motifs seem to him to epitomize the poetic and musical structures. Whether or not these correspondences were intended by Debussy, they may well be useful for more than a few of his admirers. But critical interpretations are as uncertain as the faun's memories, and there will be other interpretations to draw us on toward the happiness of enjoying ever more intensely both poem and music.

Backgrounds and Sources

Beyond the documents cited in the introduction to this edition, there is an endless range of material that would be relevant to a study of Debussy's *Prelude*. The following selections include more extensive writings that are referred to only briefly in the introduction, and several additional ones that are helpful in showing the interaction of the arts in Debussy's time. Unless specified otherwise, all numbered footnotes in the following material are those of the author.

THÉODORE DE BANVILLE

[Wagner, Poetry, and Music, 1869]†

Théodore de Banville (1823–91) was a great master of poetry and drama, contemporary and friend of Baudelaire, early admirer of Mallarmé's *Faun*, and a favorite of Debussy's during his student years. Debussy's songs with Banville texts, and his unfinished opera based on Banville's *Diane au bois*, together with the testimony of friends, suggest that he quite likely read Banville's report of Wagner's early opera *Rienzi* (written on the occasion of its first Paris performance, at the Théâtre Lyrique, April 12, 1869), though the younger men, Mallarmé and Debussy, were naturally inclined to neglect this work in favor of Wagner's later ones. Banville's chief modern interpreter, Eileen Souffrin-Le Breton, has devoted four articles to his connections with our interests: *Une amitié de poètes: Théodore de Banville et Stéphane Mallarmé*, in *Le Goéland (Paramé)*, June 1943; *Théodore de Banville et la musique*, in *Oxford French Studies*, IX (1955), 238; *Debussy lecteur de Banville*, in *Revue de musicologie*, XLVI (1960), 200; *Théodore de Banville, inspirateur des musiciens*, in *Le Bayou (Houston)*, XCV (1963), 469.

* * * Richard Wagner * * * has long renounced the division of his operas into cavatinas, duos, and terzettos; he wishes to have a continuous melody, coming to birth, living, and dying with the action that it embraces and clings to; this melody should be the very soul of the poem, now struggling, now oppressed, now desperate, now triumphant, but never ceasing to be one and to keep us in the ideal atmosphere where the poet has conveyed us with him; its various parts, connected by supple transitions, should form a single body, a powerful and marvelous unity. Melody is everything in Wagner's music. He could say correctly, in speaking of his opponents, "They derive their idea of melody from works in which alongside melody there are passages without any melody, which serve above all to put the melody as they understand it into the light that

† Banville, *Critiques*, Paris, 1917, pp. 174–76, 178–80. Translation by the editor.

is so dear to them."

There is the whole question. The revolution attempted by Richard Wagner, far from being bizarre, as it is thought to be, is not at all bizarre. In the aristocratic Italian idea, which we have adopted from Italy, an opera is a series of arias, duos, cavatinas, between which a sort of noise absolutely devoid of character allows for conversation, for refreshments, and for exchanging visits. On the contrary, Wagner the democrat, the new man, wanting to write for all and for the people, understands music drama as a harmonious whole in which all the arts—poetry, music, painting, and sculpture, by the disposition of groups and of scenery—make essential contributions to the drama, competing to dominate, to seize, to spellbind the soul of the spectator, of the listener, and to cause in him a lasting, deep impression. It is curious to hear Eugène Delacroix and Edgar Poe claim, one for painting and the other for poetry, this same unity of melody that Wagner also claims, and to hear them assert in terms which are almost identical with his that it is the vital, essential condition of their art. And who does not know that these arts are similar?

Richard Wagner, and this is the other side of his revolution, does not admit, or rather does not understand, that Poetry and Music, these two sisters who are the two halves—or better, the two aspects—of the same art, should have lived so long as two hostile sisters, scorning and despising each other, and united like two convicts by a heavy chain that they can hardly bear. For him, to say Poetry is to say Music, and when music speaks alone, it is to paint the *beyond,* the *unexpressed,* that which human speech, even in rhythm, is incapable of translating; for the ineffable privilege of music is to say what cannot be said, the things that go beyond our intelligence and that are understood directly by our soul. "Music of the future" someone has said of this intimate, strict, absolute union between the two forms of human thought whose glorious symbol is the Lyre; one might have said as well "music of the past," for I imagine that Orpheus, celebrating the glory of the gods, the life of the plants, and the souls of the stones, did not create his verse and his melody separately, but that verse and melody, born, thought, created together, trembled at once on the lyre whose sounds soothed the tigers and the rocks. The rocks, to be sure, are only hard, and the tigers are only wild. When the ode sounds out, no longer cold and silent but having recovered its heavenly voice, let us say no more "music of the past" nor "music of the future"; what must be said is: Music. * * *

FRANCIS GRIERSON

[An American at Mallarmé's Salons, 1889–92]†

Grierson was a self-taught pianist and improvisor, who came from America to Europe as a young man in 1869, toured with great success, and then gave up music to become a writer. His most famous book is a memoir of the 1850s in Illinois, *The Valley of Shadows*, Boston, 1909. For further information on his extraordinary life and work, see Harold P. Simonson, *Francis Grierson*, New York, 1966, and Arthur Farwell, *Francis Grierson—Musical Liberator*, in *Musical America*, XIX (Dec. 13, 1913), 19. Paul Bourget, the poet with whom Grierson contrasts Mallarmé, was the author of "Beau soir," one of Debussy's first songs.

* * *

My first visit to Stéphane Mallarmé was made one day just after leaving the house of M. Paul Bourget; and I seldom think of the poet without also thinking of the novelist.

To go from the residence of M. Bourget to that of Mallarmé was like going from one city to another. From the Faubourg Saint-Germain to the Rue de Rome one passes from a world of conventional refinement to a quarter of Paris with no historic or social interest. Independent, both in the intellectual and the material sense of the word, M. Bourget chose that part of the city which suited his tastes. Mallarmé had to live not where he pleased, but where he could. The street inhabited by the novelist was flanked by old walls, behind which lay the mansions of the old nobility; and the interior of his residence was in keeping with the customs and the modes of the neighbourhood. Subdued in tone, yet richly furnished, the place had the air of refinement which one is accustomed to see in the houses of the conservative aristocracy.

† Grierson, *Parisian Portraits*, London, 1913, pp. 83–98. Reprinted by permission of The Bodley Head Limited.

It always gives one pleasure to see artists and writers living in comfort, removed from the noise and distractions of the world; but I found Mallarmé living in a house that resembled thousands of other houses. There was no distinctive character in anything, except in the man himself. M. Bourget is a personal power in his writings. Mallarmé showed his power in manner, disposition, and personal charm. Without his personality his literature alone would hardly have attracted so many writers of different schools.

Mallarmé's reception room was so small that a company of fifteen persons filled it. Yet, to this little room, containing nothing but a centre table and chairs, came the intellectual youth of France, representing every school and social grade—future academicians, deputies, diplomats, novelists, editors, historians, and composers, the visitors being of all ages, but principally under thirty.

The yoke of officialdom lies heavy on the neck of genius. Mallarmé was one of the few who remained independent. But even in this he did not try,—it was the nature of the man. To see him stand by the fireplace rolling a cigarette, talking in a low voice, half to himself, half to his visitors, was to see a man free from conventional bondage. And it was like arriving at a cool mountain-spring after a long tramp through a burning desert. The visitor came here without fear, hindrance, or hypocrisy. The body rested while the spirit was being refreshed. There was neither loud talk, discussion, attempt at wit, nor striving after effect. This little room was the one place in Paris where the soul could manifest itself in freedom. Everywhere else pose and persiflage were in order. Any one coming here with the airs of a patron would, in a few moments, settle down in his seat, subdued, transformed by the serenity of the place.

Once I witnessed the arrival of an obstreperous visitor; but Mallarmé, with his usual easy manner, let silence bring about the miracle of subjugation. The visitor, once seated, was soon overcome by the collective calm. When he tried to lead the conversation the host allowed him to talk for a time, then, turning to M. Henri de Régnier, sitting in the corner by the fireside, he addressed him in an undertone, thus adroitly shifting the loud talker to one side. This was the only salon where a company dared to sit for any time without a clatter of words. In the other salons animated conversation was considered the correct thing; without it people would feel troubled or bored; at other houses it was the custom for visitors to seek the acquaintance of other visitors, the host in many cases being, like Leconte de Lisle, incapable of holding the attention of a company.

Whistler and Manet have pictured Mallarmé at two periods of his life. Whistler's subtle portrait suggests the apparition of an extraordinary personality between two epochs—the old and the new. Time, like a dream, has settled over his features as the mists of twilight over an enchanted landscape; there is a suggestion of a poetic veil separating him from the world like the smoke from his cigarette, which, he said, he used as a screen between himself and the crowd.

In Manet's canvas the poet is younger and reminds one of Deroy's portrait of Baudelaire. The expression is anxious and the figure restless; the conflict between the poetic and the material is at its height; he has not yet learned how to discard the perplexing, dismiss the puerile, enter the sanctuary of his own gods and abide contented there. For the truth is that, although Mallarmé was born in Paris, and had experienced the innovations of the Second Empire, the Third Republic, the bourgeois realism of Zola, the pretensions of unoriginal minds like the Goncourts, and the irony of critics like M. Jules Lemaître, he belonged to the *ancien régime*. Mallarmé was an intellectual aristocrat. His tranquil dignity, spiritual poise, politeness without hypocrisy or affectation, his freedom from the usual vulgarities of a society skilled in the art of sensation and puffery, made him conspicuous. But there was method in the obscurity of his literary manner. He was obscure with a purpose. He would make it an impossibility for the critic *à la mode*, be he a Brunetière or a Lemaître, to scale the barriers of his poetic domain.

When I first knew Mallarmé, in 1889, the official professors were in a strange state of ignorance respecting his influence. Here was a man, living very near the borders of actual want, exercising a power which no millionaire could claim. Here was an intellectual magnet that attracted other intellects, causing young poets, artists, and journalists to mount four flights of stairs once a week to sit and listen to what words might fall from the lips of the master. He drew them towards him, not by his will, but by his influence. He never made an effort to induce a visitor to return, never flattered, never tried to be more amiable to one than to another.

Bourget was independent, but Mallarmé was even more so. Let us not be blinded by appearances—the gifted novelist, living in aristocratic seclusion in the Faubourg Saint-Germain, could not attain such privacy without much care and effort. He was in Paris, but not of it. Mallarmé, the poet and dreamer, was not only in Paris, but a vital part of its intellectual life. A Socrates in the world of symbols, he might as well have lived in a tent or sat in the market-place; for, with him, art and life were in no way connected with the fashionable world.

* * *

There was a notion prevalent that Mallarmé's salon was frequented exclusively by poets and artists of the symbolical school; but I soon realised the folly of believing in hearsay evidence. His visitors represented all the schools of the day; and it is easy to understand the jealousy of some of the Sorbonne professors who saw young authors of talent doing homage to a man who paid no heed to the examples of the academicians. It was but natural that "official" professors should pretend that Stéphane Mallarmé was without serious influence. Their attitude was, in part, the result of ignorance. Who has ever met with an official professor who gave himself the trouble to learn the truth by seeing the outside world with his own eyes, and hearing its voices with his own ears?

It was by visiting this salon many times, during a period of several years, that I arrived at the truth. I learned, after repeated visits, what a far-reaching influence went forth from this obscure room. Little did the professors at the Sorbonne know of this ascendency, revolving, as they were, in their own limited circle which they mistook for the universe. Louis XVI imagined that the taking of the Bastille was an insignificant street brawl. How could he know what was going on in Paris when he spent his time at Versailles? The people were taking power out of his hands; he was not among them; he could not see the truth. At a time when academicians were ridiculing Mallarmé, he, without trying, was undermining the old edifice with hundreds of disciples, many of whom had been the cleverest students in the *lycées* of the Latin Quarter. Some of these young men were already acknowledged journalists of talent, others would become critics, playwrights, politicians.

So great was the outcry in 1889 and the following years that the question of abolishing the Académie Française was freely discussed, many deputies taking sides with the young writers of the advanced schools. It needed only a few visits to Mallarmé's salon to convince me that here was the one vital force operating in the literary world of Paris. Renan was lecturing at the Sorbonne; Mallarmé was rolling cigarettes and talking nonchalantly to visitors at his own fireside. Renan, the giant, spoke from an official platform, but the poet of the Rue de Rome was now the man of power.

What illusions float about the academical chair! It is surprising that writers of independent means put themselves to so much humiliation to enter the Académie. When Renan became a candidate he began the course of official visits and found himself one evening at the dinner-table of Victor Hugo. The guests talked freely, but Renan sat like a timid schoolboy, with his eyes cast down, giving the réplique to Hugo in four words: "Oui, maître; non, maître"; not daring to go further for fear of offending the host, and so losing his vote.

The sphere of a writer's influence is fixed. Every soul has its own world. But sometimes one writer brings to mind another. In his personality Mallarmé made me think of Whitman and his artless simplicity and unaffected sincerity. But the features of the French poet were unlike any other poet or writer, living or dead. There was nothing eccentric about his face or his person, and he never put on evening dress to receive his visitors. His receptions were for men, and the poet appeared in the clothes he had worn during the day. In this he also reminded me of Walt Whitman, whom I saw in Washington in 1868. Mallarmé opened the door himself for his guests when they arrived, and went to the door with them when they left. I never saw him sit in the presence of his company. This might have led to some clatter among the guests. The guests came to hear Mallarmé, not to talk among themselves.

At first I was not aware of the real nature of these evenings. Once I noticed that when one guest addressed another no reply was given; conversation between the guests was therefore impossible. M. Henri de Régnier, who on each occasion occupied the same seat in the corner at the host's right, was always silent. He seemed to be the guest of honour. Mallarmé frequently addressed his conversation to him, but M. de Régnier was not there to talk, but to listen; instead of replying he simply took a few extra whiffs of his cigarette. Every one understood.

To a philosophical mind these evenings were so many lessons in the virtue of silence. No one tried to make the poet speak; he himself never tried to make others speak. And yet these evenings were full of instruction and charm. Thought came as in a Quaker meeting, with this difference: Mallarmé was the presiding Quaker who never sat down. He occupied the floor by the will of the guests. Here one learned the true value of silence in affairs of the intellect. Everything that is made up for the occasion belongs to the puerile and the trivial. The talk imposed by self-interest and vanity is never edifying. If you wish to influence others be natural; let Nature have a hand in your talk and your receptions.

Mallarmé owed much to his sojourn in England in his earlier years. Here he entered into the spirit and substance of English poetry, and attained that extra something which he needed to embellish the exclusiveness and delicacy in his nature which later made him such an ardent admirer of Poe.

I saw Mallarmé alone on several occasions. "Poe," he remarked, on one of these visits, "I regard as an Irish genius transplanted to America."

"Hugo," I said, at another time, "advises writers never to dream."

"He is wrong," answered Mallarmé; "dreams have as much influence as actions."

And truth to say, this dreamer of dreams exercised a power seldom attained by any Frenchman before or during his day. Everything comes to him who seeks for nothing. The dreamer contents himself in a world of meditation and contemplation; his ideas are many, but his words are few. He dislikes action, yet he attracts the active. He seeks no réclames, yet he is acclaimed. In a study of Mallarmé and his salon, which appeared in 1892, I said: "In this poet we find a philosopher free from superstition and prejudice, a thinker who embraces all that is vital in art, music, and literature."

The best minds are often led into foolish acts, even against their better judgment; and the poet was inveigled into accepting a banquet in his honour, offered by a number of his admirers, at which conventional toasts, speeches, and responses, prearranged and machine-made, were the order of the evening. He was proclaimed "prince" of the young poets; but Mallarmé sat immovable, fatigued, and bored. It was no place for him.

When a wise man is placed in a ridiculous position, the fools, as Goethe says, have their innings. We blunder the moment we cease to reason and permit others to reason for us. Mallarmé, who was king in his own sphere, cut a poor figure at his banquet. In this attitude the poet descended to the arena of strife, on a level with others of not half his merit who had dinners given in their honour.

How difficult it is to refuse at the right moment! The art of saying "No" is the supreme art in the life of every thinker. Of all things connected with the daily routine of a man of talent, this thing of knowing when and how to refuse is the simplest and the rarest. It is so easy to know and so hard to do. But until we learn to do it we can expect nothing but misunderstanding and failure.

It was remarked by a journalist that Mallarmé, at this banquet, looked as if he had come to bury his last friend. And no wonder; for he had descended from his sanctuary in the Rue de Rome to a place where his star gave no light. He was attracted beyond his orbit by the comets and meteors of the phenomenal world, and he could say with Joseph Roux: "When I return from the country of men I take with me illusions and disillusions."

STÉPHANE MALLARMÉ[†]

The Evolution of Literature (1891)
[Interview with Jules Huret]

Besides his most famous poem, *L'Après-midi d'un faune*, Stéphane Mallarmé (1842–98) wrote translations of the poems of Edgar Allan Poe; another long poem *Hérodiade*, which Paul Hindemith was to use as the basis of his ballet for Martha Graham; a later poem, *Un Coup de dès*, remarkable for its new departures in syntax and typography; and many splendid shorter poems, some of which provided texts for songs by Debussy, Ravel, and other composers. Mallarmé's essays, collected under the characteristic title of *Divagations*, are profound discussions of poetry, full of references to music, which he views jealously from a point of view that is not to be located precisely without a sustained study of several of his works. The literature about Mallarmé includes many special studies of his relations to music, which are listed in the bibliography, p. 167 and footnote 5, p. 5, above.

(Stéphane Mallarmé: One of the most generally beloved men of letters, along with Catulle Mendès. Average height; pointed beard turning

[†] From Mallarmé, *Selected Prose Poems, Essays, and Letters*, translated and with an introduction by Bradford Cook, Baltimore, 1956. Reprinted by permission of The Johns Hopkins Press and Editions Gallimard.

grey; large straight nose; long, pointed ears like those of a satyr; wide-open eyes of extraordinary brilliance; an unusual expression of finesse tempered by the appearance of great goodness. Whenever he speaks, his words are accompanied by rhythmical gestures full of grace, precision, and eloquence. His voice drags a little at the end of his words and becomes gradually gentler. There is great charm in this man. You feel that there is an incorruptible pride in him which lifts him above all things; the pride of a god or seer. And once this is felt, inwardly and instinctively you bow down before him).

"We are now witnessing a spectacle," he told me, "which is truly extraordinary, unique in the history of poetry: every poet is going off by himself with his own flute, and playing the songs he pleases. For the first time since the beginning of poetry, poets have stopped singing bass. Hitherto, as you know, if they wished to be accompanied, they had to be content with the great organ of official meter. Well, it was simply overplayed and they got tired of it! I am sure that when the great Hugo died, he was convinced that he had buried all poetry for the next century; and yet Paul Verlaine had already written *Sagesse*. We can forgive Hugo his illusion, when we remember all the miracles he produced; he was simply forgetting the eternal instinct, the perpetual and unavoidable growth of the lyrical. But the essential and undeniable point is this: that in a society without stability, without unity, there can be no stable or definitive art. From that incompletely organized society—which also explains the restlessness of certain minds—the unexplained need for individuality was born. The literary manifestations of today are in a direct reflection of that need.

"A more immediate explanation of recent innovations is this: it has finally been understood that the old verse form was *not* the absolute, unique, and changeless form, but just one way to be sure of writing good verse. We say to children: 'Don't steal, and you'll be honest.' That is true, but it is not everything. Is it possible to write poetry without reference to time-honored precepts? Poets have answered this question affirmatively, and I believe that they are right. Poetry is everywhere in language, so long as there is rhythm—everywhere except on posters and the back page of the newspaper. In the genre we call 'prose,' there are verses—sometimes admirable verses—of all sorts of rhythms. Actually, there is no such thing as prose: there is the alphabet, and then there are verses which are more or less closely knit, more or less diffuse. So long as there is stylistic effort, there is versification.

"I said a minute ago that today's poetry is, in the main, the result of the poets' boredom with official verse. Even the partisans of official verse share this boredom. Isn't it rather abnormal that, when we open a book of poetry, we should be sure of finding uniform and conventional rhythms throughout? And yet, all the while, the writer hopes to arouse our interest in the essential variety of human feelings! Where is the inspiration in all this! Where is the unforeseen! How tiresome it all is! Official verse must be used only in the crisis moments of the soul. Modern poets have understood this. With a fine sense of the delicate and the sparing, they hover around the official alexandrine, approach it with unusual timidity, almost with fear; and rather than use it as their principle or as a point of departure, they suddenly conjure it up, and with it they crown their poem or period!

"Moreover, the same transformation has taken place in music. Instead of the very clearly delineated melodies of the past, we have an infinity of broken melodies which enrich the poetic texture, and we no longer have the impression of strong cadence."

"Is that how the scission was effected?" I asked.

"Why, yes. The Parnassians were fond of a very formal prosody which has its own beauty, and they failed to realize that the modern poets were simply complementing their work; this also had the advantage of creating a sort of interregnum for the noble alexandrine which had been at bay, crying for mercy. What we have to realize is that the most recent poetical writings do not tend to suppress the official verse; they tend rather to let a little more air into the poem, to create a kind of fluidity or mobility between long-winded verses, which has heretofore been lacking. In an orchestra, for example, you may suddenly hear very fine bursts of sound from the basses; but you know perfectly well that if there were nothing but that, you would soon have enough of it. Young poets space these bursts so that they will occur only when a total effect is to be produced. In this way, the alexandrine (which was invented by nobody, but rather poured forth spontaneously from the instrument of language) will get out of its present finicky, sedentary state, and henceforth it will be freer, more sudden, more refreshed. Its value will lie exclusively in its use during the soul's most serious times. And future volumes of poetry will be traversed by a majestic first verse which scatters in its wake an infinity of motifs originating in the individual's sensibility.

"So there has been scission because both sides have been unaware that their points of view are reconcilable rather than mutually destructive. On the one hand, the Parnassians have, in effect, been perfectly obedient servants of verse, and have sacrificed their personalities. The young poets, on the other hand, have anchored their instinct in a variety of modes, as if there were no precedent; actually, all they are doing is reducing here and there the stiffness of the Parnassian structures; and it seems to me that the two points of view are complementary.

"Despite all this, I still believe, personally, that, with the miraculous knowledge of verse and with the superb instinct for rhythmic pause which such masters as Banville possess, the alexandrine can be infinitely varied and can reproduce all possible shades of human passion. Banville's *Forgeron*, for example, has a number of alexandrines which seem interminable, yet others which are unbelievably concise.

"But, after all, it was a good thing to give our perfect and traditional poetic instrument a little rest. It had been overworked."

"So much for form," I said. "What about content?"

"As far as content is concerned," he answered, "I feel that the young poets are nearer than the Parnassians to the poetic ideal. The latter still treat their subjects as the old philosophers and orators did: that is, they present things directly, whereas I think that they should be presented allusively. Poetry lies in the *contemplation* of things, in the image emanating from the reveries which things arouse in us. The Parnassians take something in its entirety and simply exhibit it; in so doing, they fall short of mystery; they fail to give our minds that exquisite joy which consists of believing that we are creating something. To *name* an object is largely to destroy poetic enjoyment, which comes from gradual divination. The ideal is to *suggest* the object. It is the perfect use of this mystery which constitutes symbol. An object must be gradually evoked in order to show a state of soul; or else, choose an object and from it elicit a state of soul by means of a series of decodings."

"Now," I said, "we are coming to the big objection I was going to make: obscurity!"

"Yes, it is a dangerous thing," he replied, "regardless of whether it results from the reader's inadequacy or from the poet's. But if you avoid the work it involves, you are cheating. If a person of mediocre intelligence and insufficient literary experience happens to open an obscure book and insists on enjoying it, something is wrong; there has simply been a misunderstanding. There must always be enigma in poetry. The purpose of literature—the *only* purpose—is to *evoke* things."

"Was it you, sir," I asked, "who created the new movement in poetry?"

"I detest 'schools,'" he replied, "and anything resembling schools. The professorial attitude toward literature is repugnant to me. Literature is entirely an individual matter. As far as I am concerned, a poet today, in the midst of this society which refuses to let him live, is a man who seeks out solitude in order to sculpture his own tomb. The reason I appear to be the leader of a school, is, first of all, that I have always taken an interest in the ideas of young poets; and second, because of my sincerity in recognizing the originality of what the latest writers have contributed. In reality, I am a hermit. I believe that poetry should be for the supreme pomp and circumstance of a constituted society in which glory should have its place. Most people seem to have forgotten glory. In our time the poet can only go on strike against society, and turn his back on all the contaminated ways and means that are offered him. For anything that is offered him is necessarily inferior to his ideal and to his secret labor."

I then asked Mallarmé what Verlaine's position would be in the history of this poetic movement.

"He was the first to react against the impeccable and impassible Parnassian attitudes. His fluid verse and certain of his intentional dissonances were already evident in *Sagesse*. Later on, around 1875, all the Parnassians (except for a few friends such as Mendès, Dierx, and Cladel) shrieked with horror at my *Afternoon of a Faun,* and, all together, they threw it out. For I *was* trying, actually, to make a sort of running pianistic commentary upon the fully preserved and dignified alexandrine—a sort of musical accompaniment which the poet composes himself, so that the official verse will appear only on the really important occasions. But the father, the real father of all the young poets is Verlaine, the magnificent Verlaine. The attitude of the man is just as noble as the attitude of the writer. For it is the only possible attitude at a time when all poets are outlaws. Think of absorbing all the grief that he has—and with his pride and his tremendous pluck!"

"What do you think of the end of Naturalism?"

"Up to now, writers have entertained the childish belief that if they could just choose a certain number of precious stones, for example, and put the names on paper, they would be *making* precious stones. Now, really! that is impossible, no matter how well it is done. Poetry consists of *creation:* we must delve into our souls for states and gleams of such perfect purity, so perfectly sung and illuminated, that they will truly be the jewels of man. When we do that, we have symbol, we have creation, and the word 'poetry' has its full meaning. This, in short, is the only possible human creation. And if, in fact, the precious stones we wear do *not* show a state of soul, they are improperly worn. Take women, for example, eternal thieves that they are. . . .

"And just think," he added, chuckling; "the marvelous thing about jewelry stores is that, occasionally, we learn from the chief of police that what the woman wore improperly was something she didn't know the secret meaning of—something, therefore, which didn't belong to her.

"But to get back to Naturalism. It seems to me that when we use that word, we mean the work of Émile Zola; and when he has finished his work, the name will disappear. I have great admiration for Zola. Actually, what he does is not so much literature as evocative art. He depends as little as possible on literary means. True, he uses words, but that is all. Everything else is based on his marvelous sense of organization and has immediate repercussions in the mind of the mob. His talent is truly powerful; consider his tremendous feeling for life, his mob movements, that texture in Nana's skin that every one of us has touched; and he paints it all with prodigious colors. It really is an admirably organized piece of work. But literature is more of an intellectual thing than that. Things already exist, we don't have to create them; we simply have to see their relationships. * * *

From *Music and Literature* (*1894*)

* * *

Except for study-sheets, rubrics, parchment, and such, I consider reading to be a hopeless occupation. So it is that all attempts at the manufacture of happiness have failed for lack of proper means. I know of cases in which even the most secret and careful of such means cannot, must not, satisfy us.

Something else! yes, it is as if the chance trembling of a page sought only hesitation and fluttered with impatience at the possibility of— something else. We know, of course, that we are subject to the absolute law which states that only what exists exists. Yet it would be obviously

From *Music and Literature (1894)*

inconsistent to choose such an empty pretext as the basis for refusing all delusion, for we would then be refusing the very pleasure that we seek. The *beyond* is our means to that pleasure; I might almost say the "instrument" of our pleasure were it not repugnant to me to disassemble fiction in public (for it would be blasphemous to analyze the "mechanics" of literature and thus discover its chief cog—which is, in any case, nothingness). Yes, for me the miracle occurs when, in a dream of fiction, we seize the ideal which is absent here below, yet explosively present up above, and hurl it to some forbidden, thunderbolt height of heaven.

Why should we do this?

It is a game.

For just as we have the right to elicit emptiness from ourselves (hampered as we may be by reality too solidly, too preponderantly enthroned in us), so do we act that a sublime attraction may lovingly deliver us from that reality—and yet be filled with it and shed glittering lights upon it through empty space and in willful, solitary celebrations.

As for myself, I ask no less of literature. And now I am going to prove my point.

Nature exists; She will not be changed, although we may add cities, railroads, or other inventions to our material world.

Therefore, our eternal and only problem is to seize relationships and intervals, however few or multiple. Thus, faithful to some special vision deep within, we may extend or simplify the world at will.

To create is to conceive an object in its fleeting moment, in its absence.

To do this, we simply compare its facets and dwell lightly, negligently upon their multiplicity. We conjure up a scene of lovely, evanescent, intersecting forms. We recognize the entire and binding arabesque thus formed as it leaps dizzily in terror or plays disquieting chords; or, through a sudden digression (by no means disconcerting), we are warned of its likeness unto itself even as it hides. Then when the melodic line has given way to silence, we seem to hear such themes as are the very logic and substance of our soul. Yet whatever the agony may be in which the Monster writhes (as, through Her golden wounds, She pours the proof that She is always entire, always Herself), no vanquished throe may bend or cross the omnipresent Line which runs infinitely from point to point in Its creation of idea—creation perhaps unseen by man, mysterious, like some Harmony of perfect purity.

I am convinced that the constant grasp and realization of this ideal constitutes our obligation to Him Who once unleashed Infinity—Whose rhythm (as our fingers longingly seek it out among the keys of our verbal instrument) can be rendered by the fitting words of our daily tongue.

For in truth, what is Literature if not our mind's ambition (in the form of language) to define things; to prove to the satisfaction of our soul that a natural phenomenon corresponds to our imaginative understanding of it. And our hope, of course, is that we may ourselves be reflected in it.

I know that Music—at least in the usual sense of the word: that is, concert performances with strings, brass, wood winds, and occasionally libretti—has a similar though unexpressed ambition (She is never very confiding). And when, a moment ago, I was sketching those winding and mobile variations of the Idea which are the prerogative of the written word, some of you may have been reminded of certain orchestral phrasings in which we hear, first, a withdrawal to the shades, swirls and uneasy hesitation, and then suddenly the bursting, leaping, multiple ecstasy of Brilliance, like the approaching radiance of a sunrise. Yet this will all be useless until language, retempered and purified by the flight of song, has given it meaning.

So now we are reaching the end of our search. There can be—or rather there *must* be—an exchange following this triumphant contribution of Music: the written word must rise and Music must receive it for a brief plaintive space, else the efficacies of life will be blind to their own brilliance, hidden, and without release. I am asking for a total restoration, in perfect and neutral silence, whereby the mind may seek its own native land again: let us have quakes and slippings, unlimited and unerring trajectories, rich revery in sudden flight, delightful unfulfillment, some special lunge or synthesis. But let there be no sonorous tumult which could be resorbed in dreams.

The greatest and most magical writers have always realized this ambition.

These, then, will be the precise and reciprocal elements of Mystery in our possession (we can forget the old distinction between Music and Literature—the one purposely separated from the other in preparation for their ultimate meeting): Music will release the powers lying within that abstract center of hearing, and even of vision, which is Comprehension; while Comprehension, in all its spaciousness, will lend equal power to the printed page.

I suggest, at my own esthetic risk, the following conclusion (and if

I were fortunate enough to win your silent approval of it, I should feel fully honored this evening): namely, that Music and Literature constitute the moving facet—now looming toward obscurity, now glittering unconquerably—of that single, true phenomenon which I have called Idea.

The one bends toward the other, submerges, then returns to the surface with its treasure; another dive, another fluctuation, and the entire cycle is created to perfection. For humanity in general, this will be done theatrically: they will sit unconsciously and hear a performance of their own greatness. The individual, on the other hand, will be enlightened by the book, his teacher and constant companion.

* * *

From *Crisis in Poetry* (*1895*)

A fundamental and fascinating crisis in literature is now at hand.

Such is the plain and present truth in the eyes of all those for whom literature is of primary importance. What we are witnessing as the finale of our own century is not upheaval (as was the case a hundred years ago), but rather a fluttering in the temple's veil—meaningful folds and even a little tearing.

This is disconcerting for the French reading public, whose habits were interrupted by the death of Victor Hugo. Pursuing his mysterious task, Hugo reduced all prose—philosophy, oratory, history—to poetry; and since he was himself poetry personified, he nearly abolished the philosopher's, speaker's, or historian's right to self-expression. In that wasteland, with silence all around, he was a monument. Yet in a crypt of equal silence lay the divinity of this majestic, unconscious idea: namely, that the form we call verse is itself, quite simply, literature; that we have verse so long as we have diction, rhythm so long as we have style. Poetry, I think, waited patiently and respectfully until this giant (whose ever more grasping, ever firmer blacksmith's hand was coming to be the definition of verse) had disappeared; then it broke up. The entire language was fitted out for prosody, and therein it re-discovered its vital sense of pause. Now it could fly off, freely scattering its numberless and irreducible elements. Or we might well compare it to the multiple sounds issuing from a purely verbal orchestration.

That was the beginning of the change in poetry which Verlaine, with his fluid verse, had secretly and unexpectedly prepared when he returned to certain primitive resources in language.

I was witness to this adventure. And although my role in it was not so influential as has been claimed (for no single person was responsible), I did at least take great interest in it. It is time to discuss it, and it seems better to do so at a distance, or, so to speak, anonymously.

It will be agreed that because of the priority on magic power which is given to rhyme, French poetry has been intermittent ever since its evolution. It shines for a moment, dies out, and waits. There is extinction—or rather wear and tear which reveal the weft; there is repetition. After an almost century-long period of poetic orgy and excess which can be compared only to the Renaissance, the latest poetic urge (counteracting a number of different circumstances) is being fulfilled not by a darkening or cooling off process, but, on the contrary, by a variation in continuing brilliance. The retempering of verse, ordinarily a secret affair, is now being done openly: poets are resorting to delightful approximations.

The kind of treatment that has been given to the hieratic canon of verse can, I think, be divided into three graduated parts.

Official prosody has cut and dried rules; there lies its obstinacy. It gives its official approval to such "wise" procedures as the observance of the hemistich, and pronounces judgment on the slightest effort to simulate versification. It is like the law which states, for example, that abstinence from theft is the essence of honesty. But this is precisely what we need least to learn; for if we have not understood it by ourselves from the first, it is useless to obey it.

Those who are still faithful to the alexandrine, i.e., to the modern hexameter, have gone inside it and loosened this rigid, childish metrical mechanism; and so, now that such artificial metronomes have been abolished, there is joy for our ears alone in perceiving all possible combinations and interrelationships of twelve tones.

Consider the most recent literary taste.

Here is a rather typical and interesting example of it.

Henri de Régnier, a poet of great tact, still considers the alexandrine to be *the* gem—a gem, however, which (like sword or flower) he discloses but rarely, and even then only with some well-considered pattern in mind. He disturbs this verse form only with the greatest circumspection; he hovers and plays around it, yields to its related harmonies, and finally shows it forth in all its pride and purity. His fingering may fail at the eleventh syllable, or often linger on to a thirteenth. He excels in such accompaniments, which are, of course, the delicate, proud invention of his own original talent; they point up the temporary uneasiness of those who play the traditional poetic instrument. We discover a quite different example of knowing disobedience in the case of Jules Laforgue, who, in the beginning, abandoned the old worn-out form and initiated us in the secret and unfailing charm of defective verse.

Up to now, therefore (as shown in the two examples just mentioned), there has been either the delicacy of a Régnier or the self-indulgence of a Laforgue in metrical treatment, as a result of the fatigue brought on by the abuse of our national rhythm. That rhythm, like the national flag, must be used sparingly. There has, however, been one interesting exception: an occasional and wilful disobedience in the form of beautifully executed dissonances for the sensitive ear. And to think that, scarcely fifteen years ago, pedants that we are, we would have been outraged by this phenomenon—as if it were an illiterate's sacrilege! Let me say, finally, that the official alexandrine, like a memory, haunts about these rhythmic variations and thus adds to their luster.

Modern free verse—unlike the seventeenth-century free verse, which we find in fables or operas, and which was simply an arrangement of various well-known meters ungoverned by strophes—derives its entire originality from what we may properly call its "polymorphic" character. And the breaking up of official verse should now be what the poets will, should even be endless, provided there is pleasure to be had in it. For example, there might be a certain euphony which the reader's own poetic instinct could fragmentize with a sort of native and unerring accuracy (such has been the recent verse of Moréas). Or perhaps a rhythmical gesture of languor and revery, or of startled passion (as in the work of Vielé-Griffin). Prior to these, there was Kahn's very skillful notation of the tonal values of words. But these are only a few of the names; there are others equally typical; Charles Morice, Verhaeren, Dujardin, Mockel, etc., whose works should be consulted; they will bear out what I have said.

But the truly remarkable fact is this: for the first time in the literary history of any nation, along with the general and traditional great organ of orthodox verse which finds its ecstasy on an ever-ready keyboard, any poet with an individual technique and ear can build his own instrument, so long as his fluting, bowing, or drumming are accomplished—play that instrument and dedicate it, along with others, to Language.

Thus we have won a great new freedom; and it is my firm belief that no beauty of the past has been destroyed as a result. I am convinced that the solemn poetic tradition which was mainly established by our classical genius will continue to be observed on all important occasions. But whenever it shall seem unfitting to disturb the echoes of that venerable past for sentimental or narrative purposes, we shall be careful to avoid such disturbance. Each soul is a melody; its strands must be bound up. Each poet has his flute or viol, with which to do so.

In my opinion, we have been late in finding the true condition and possibility not only of poetic self-expression, but of free and individual modulation.

Languages are imperfect because multiple; the supreme language is missing. Inasmuch as thought consists of writing without pen and paper, without whispering even, without the sound of the immortal Word, the diversity of languages on earth means that no one can utter words which would bear the miraculous stamp of Truth Herself Incarnate. This is clearly nature's law—we stumble on it with a smile of resignation—to the effect that we have no sufficient reason for equating ourselves with God. But then, esthetically, I am disappointed when I consider how impossible it is for language to express things by means of certain keys which would reproduce their brilliance and aura—keys which do exist as a part of the instrument of the human voice, or among languages, or sometimes even in one language. When compared to the opacity of the word *ombre,* the word *ténèbres* does not seem very dark; and how frustrating the perverseness and contradiction which lend dark tones to *jour,* bright tones to *nuit!* We dream of words brilliant at once in meaning and sound, or darkening in meaning and so in sound, luminously and elementally self-succeeding. *But,* let us remember that if our dream were fulfilled, *verse would not exist*—verse which, in all its wisdom, atones for the sins of languages, comes nobly to their aid.

Strange mystery—and so, equally mysterious and meaningful, prosody sprang forth in primitive times.

The ideal would be a reasonable number of words stretched beneath our mastering glance, arranged in enduring figures, and followed by silence.

From *Crisis in Poetry* (1895)

Granted that individual inventiveness, in the case of a French poet, need not outweigh the influence of his poetic heritage; still it would be highly annoying if he were not able to follow his own paths, walk through their numberless little flowers, and gather up whatever notes his voice might find. The attempt to do so has been made just recently, and poets are still conducting learned research in the direction of syllable stressing, for example. But apart from that, there is the fascinating pastime of breaking the old alexandrine into still recognizable fragments, alternately elusive or revealing. This is preferable to total and sudden novelty. It was good to relax the rules, but the ardor which got the new school too far out of tune should now be cooled. Most delightfully out of tune, yes; but to go further, as a result of that liberation, and to suppose that every poet henceforth should invent his own prosody and base it on his own special musical gift—to say nothing of his own spelling system—is simply ridiculous. That kind of thing is cannon fodder for the newspaper boys. Verses will always be similar, and the old proportions and regularity will be observed, because the poetic act consists of our sudden realization that an idea is naturally fractionized into several motifs of equal value which must be assembled. They rhyme; and their outward stamp of authenticity is that common meter which the final stress establishes.

But the crisis in poetry lies less in the very interesting interregnum or rest treatment undergone by versification, than in certain new states of our poetic mind.

We now *hear* undeniable rays of light, like arrows gilding and piercing the meanderings of song. I mean that, since Wagner appeared, Music and Verse have combined to form Poetry.

Either one of these two elements, of course, may profitably stand apart in triumph and integrity, in a quiet concert of its own if it chooses not to speak distinctly. Or else the poem can tell of their reassociation and restrengthening: the instrumentation is brightened to the point of perfect clarity beneath the orchestral veil, while verse flies down into the evening darkness of the sounds. That modern meteor—the symphony—approaches thought with the consent or ignorance of the musician. And thought itself is no longer expressed merely in common language.

Thus Mystery bursts forth ineffably throughout the heavens of Its own impersonal magnificence, wherein it was ordained that the orchestra should complement our age-old effort to make the spoken word our only form of music.

Twin symbols interrelated.

The Decadent or Mystic Schools (as they call themselves or as they were hastily labeled by the public press) find their common meeting-ground in an Idealism which (as in the case of fugues and sonatas) shuns the materials in nature, avoids any thought that might tend to arrange them too directly or precisely, and retains only the suggestiveness of things. The poet must establish a careful relationship between two images, from which a third element, clear and fusible, will be distilled and caught by our imagination. We renounce that erroneous esthetic (even though it has been responsible for certain masterpieces) which would have the poet fill the delicate pages of his book with the actual and palpable wood of trees, rather than with the forest's shuddering or the silent scattering of thunder through the foliage. A few well-chosen sounds blown heavenward on the trumpet of true majesty will suffice to conjure up the architecture of the ideal and only habitable palace—palace of no palpable stone, else the book could not be properly closed.

It is not *description* which can unveil the efficacy and beauty of monuments, seas, or the human face in all their maturity and native state, but rather evocation, *allusion, suggestion.* These somewhat arbitrary terms reveal what may well be a very decisive tendency in modern literature, a tendency which limits literature and yet sets it free. For what is the magic charm of art, if not this: that, beyond the confines of a fistful of dust or of all other reality, beyond the book itself, beyond the very text, it delivers up that volatile scattering which we call the Spirit, Who cares for nothing save universal musicality.

Speech is not more than a commercial approach to reality. In literature, allusion is sufficient: essences are distilled and then embodied in Idea.

Song, when it becomes impalpable joy, will rise to heaven.

This is the ideal I would call Transposition; Structure is something else.

If the poem is to be pure, the poet's voice must be stilled and the initiative taken by the words themselves, which will be set in motion as they meet unequally in collision. And in an exchange of gleams they will flame out like some glittering swath of fire sweeping over precious stones, and thus replace the audible breathing in lyric poetry of old—replace the poet's own personal and passionate control of verse.

The inner structures of a book of verse must be inborn; in this way, chance will be totally eliminated and the poet will be absent. From each theme, itself predestined, a given harmony will be born somewhere in the parts of the total poem and take its proper place within the volume; because, for every sound, there is an echo. Motifs of like pattern will move in balance from point to point. There will be none of the sublime incoherence found in the page-settings of the Romantics, none of the artificial unity that used to be based on the square measurements of the book. Everything will be hesitation, disposition of parts, their alternations and relationships—all this contributing to the rhythmic totality, which will be the very silence of the poem, in its blank spaces, as that silence is translated by each structural element in its own way. (Certain recent publications have heralded this sort of book; and if we may admit their ideals as complements to our own, it must then be granted that young poets have seen what an overwhelming and harmonious totality a poem must be, and have stammered out the magic concept of the Great Work.) Then again, the perfect symmetry of verses within the poem, of poems within the volume, will extend even beyond the volume itself; and this will be the creation of many poets who will inscribe, on spiritual space, the expanded signature of genius—as anonymous and perfect as a work of art.

Chimæra, yes! And yet the mere thought of it is proof (reflected from Her scales) that during the last twenty-five years poetry has been visited by some nameless and absolute flash of lightning—like the muddied, dripping gleams on my windowpane which are washed away and brightened by streaming showers of rain—revealing that, in general, all books contain the amalgamation of a certain number of age-old truths; that actually there is only one book on earth, that it is the law of the earth, the earth's true Bible. The difference between individual works is simply the difference between individual interpretations of one true and established text, which are proposed in a mighty gathering of those ages we call civilized or literary.

Certainly, whenever I sit at concerts, amid the obscurity and ecstasy of sound, I always perceive the nascent form of some one of those poems which have their origin and dwelling in human life—a poem more understandable because unheard, because the composer, in his desire to portray its majestic lines, was not even *tempted* to "explain everything." My feeling—or my doubtlessly ineradicable prejudice as a writer—is that nothing will endure if it remains unspoken; that our present task, precisely (now that the great literary rhythms I spoke of are being broken up and scattered in a series of distinct and almost orchestrated shiverings), is to find a way of transposing the symphony to the Book: in short, to regain our rightful due. For, undeniably, the true source of Music must not be the elemental sound of brasses, strings, or wood winds, but the intellectual and written word in all its glory—Music of perfect fulness and clarity, the totality of universal relationships.

One of the undeniable ideals of our time is to divide words into two different categories: first, for vulgar or immediate, second, for essential purposes.

The first is for narrative, instruction, or description (even though an adequate exchange of human thoughts might well be achieved through the silent exchange of money). The elementary use of language involves that universal *journalistic style* which characterizes all kinds of contemporary writing, with the exception of literature.

Why should we perform the miracle by which a natural object is almost made to disappear beneath the magic waving wand of the written word, if not to divorce that object from the direct and the palpable, and so conjure up its *essence* in all purity?

When I say: "a flower!" then from that forgetfulness to which my voice consigns all floral form, something different from the usual calyces arises, something all music, essence, and softness: the flower which is absent from all bouquets.

Language, in the hands of the mob, leads to the same facility and directness as does money. But, in the Poet's hands, it is turned, above all, to dream and song; and, by the constituent virtue and necessity of an art which lives on fiction, it achieves its full efficacy.

Out of a number of words, poetry fashions a single new word which is total in itself and foreign to the language—a kind of incantation. Thus the desired isolation of language is effected; and chance (which might still have governed these elements, despite their artful and alternating renewal through meaning and sound) is thereby instantly and thoroughly abolished. Then we realize, to our amazement, that we had never truly heard this or that ordinary poetic fragment; and, at the same time, our recollection of the object thus conjured up bathes in a totally new atmosphere.

PAUL GAUGUIN

[Impressionism and After]†

Paul Gauguin (1848–1903) frequently attended Mallarmé's Tuesday evenings in the years 1889–91, after his sojourn in Martinique and before his first trip to Tahiti. He was introduced to Mallarmé by the writer Charles Morice (1861–1919), who was to provide the catalogue for the momentous Gauguin exhibition of November, 1893, then to collaborate with him on the book about his Tahitian experience, *Noa Noa*, and finally to write an important biography, from which the following citations are taken.

I think it was about 1872 when the first exhibition took place of a little group known since under the name of Impressionists. Wolves, surely, since they had no dog collars. Almost classic, yet quite simple, their pictures seemed bizarre. It was never known why. And it was madly funny. —I shall not tell their history. Everybody knows it. I recall it only to indicate one of the greatest intellectual efforts that was ever made in France, by only a few, armed with nothing but their own strength, their talent, in a fight with the formidable power of the bureaucracy, the press, and money.

* * * But this, too, is a School (another School) with all the slavery that it implies. It is another dogma.

They (the Impressionists) studied color exclusively as a decorative effect, but without liberty, stuck with likeness to a model. * * * They explored around the field of the eye, and not at the mysterious center of thought; hence they fell into scientific theories. They are the bureaucrats of tomorrow. * * *

I assure you, colored painting is entering a musical phase. Cézanne, to cite an old master, seems to be a pupil of César Franck. He continually plays the full organ, which has led me to say that he is polyphonic.

† Charles Morice, *Paul Gauguin*, Paris, 1920, pp. 149–50, 153, 152, 191–92, 201–02. Translation by the editor.

* * * Tahiti * * * The hour of the siesta has passed, the hour of burning, the dead hour.

Twilight falls. * * * They are going to sing, they are going to dance.

The men crouch at the base of the trees. The women, in the open space, as if undressed and unconcerned, rhythmically move their solid legs, their strong shoulders, their hips and their breasts, while the last rays of the sun and the first rays of the moon follow them. The voice of the men—monotone, grave, almost sad—is the orchestra of this ballet. It mingles apprehensive sighs with the flutterings of the women and their miming invitation to the love that will come with the night. * * *

[Someone protests:] "I know that no two pairs of eyes ever see identically the same reality. Yet there are limits to the interpretation of art. Here, I think these have been transgressed. There is more invention than imitation, more arbitrary despotism than fidelity, and so I have the right to dispute the whim that combines dreamlike phantasmagorias under this label: Tahiti!"

No. The artist's interpretation has no other limits than the laws of harmony.

If the artist, from his glances at the object that arouses his emotion, produces a work harmonious in each of its diverse parts as in its whole, this work is the quite faithful and quite true expression of *this* object by *this* artist, no matter how vast a divergence you observe between the *model* and the *copy*. The divergence may be more or less obvious, but there is always a divergence. For there is no art if there is no transposition. * * * It may happen that the most remote interpretation is the truest. * * *

Nature gives us only symbols—the meaning it assumes in us, the sensation, the feeling, the idea that we have of it. We possess nature only by this detour, and it is from these fictions that our reality is made. But the substance, the pretext of our fictions, is inexhaustible, eucharistic: we can all commune with its infinite richness; for everyone variously, for each fully, nature is always meaningful.

Now art—*which is within nature*—participates in this divine character. Like nature, when art is contemplated it radiates. According to the variety of minds, it multiplies. The musician can excite the painter, as the murmurs of the forest have excited the musician.

ODILON REDON

[Suggestive Art]†

Among the works of Odilon Redon (1840–1916) are marvelous drawings and prints to illustrate the works of Poe, a famous portrait of his friend Mallarmé, and many distinctive pastel paintings of flowers and dream-pictures. His writings, published only after his death, are also distinctive. His thoughts often seem very close to Debussy's. Surrealist painters of later generations claim Redon as a chief predecessor. Recent students of Debussy find Redon and his contemporaries Cézanne and Gauguin more closely related to him than the earlier "Impressionists" like Monet, with whom he has often been loosely associated. (See especially André Schaeffner's thorough study, *Debussy et ses rapports avec la peinture*, in the colloquium edited by Edith Weber, *Debussy et l'évolution de la musique au XXe siècle*, Paris, 1965, p. 151.)

Suggestive art is like an irradiation of things for the sake of the dream toward which thought also tends. Decadent or not, this is the way it is. Let us say rather that it is the growth or evolution of art toward the supreme soaring of our real life, its expansion, its highest support or moral guarantee by necessary exaltation.

This suggestive art is complete in the provocative art of music, more freely radiant. But it is in mine, too, through a combination of diverse elements gathered together, of forms transposed or transformed, without any relation of contingencies, but still having a logic. All the mistakes that the critics made about me when I began came from the fact that they did not see that nothing must be defined, nothing understood, nothing limited, nothing explained, because all that is sincerely and docilely new—like beauty—carries its meaning within itself.

Designating my drawings by giving them a title is sometimes too

† Redon, *À soi-même*, Paris, 1961, pp. 26–27. Translation by the editor. Reprinted by permission of Librairie José Corti.

much, so to speak. A title is justified only when it is vague, indeterminate, and even confusedly aiming at the equivocal. My drawings *inspire* and cannot be defined. They determine nothing. They place us, as does music, in the ambiguous world of the indeterminate.

* * * What they are then, without further explanation, which could hardly be any more precise, is this: the repercussion of a human expression, placed by innocent fantasy into an interplay of arabesques, where, I believe, the reaction in the observer's mind will inspire him to fantasies whose meanings will be great or small according to his sensibility and his imaginative ability to enlarge or diminish all things.

MAURICE DENIS

[*Decadence and Neo-Traditionalism*]†

The painter with whom Debussy's associations were actually closest was Maurice Denis (1870–1943). He began his career in the group called "Nabis," which included Bonnard, Roussel, Sérusier, Vallotton, and Vuillard; their first exhibition was in 1891. In 1893 a drawing by Denis adorned the cover of Debussy's first important publication, *La Damoiselle élue*. Denis's volume of *Théories* (1912) brings together and organizes writings of earlier years to show an evolution from symbolism to classicism in painting, remarkably analogous to a tendency in Debussy's work.

The present time is literary down to its marrow, refining on minutiæ, avid for complexities. Do you think that Botticelli in his *Primavera* intended that sickly delicacy, that sentimental affectation which we have all seen in it? Well then, work with malice, with that ulterior motive, just see what formulæ you reach!

In all times of decadence the plastic arts wither into literary affectations and naturalistic negations. * * *

From the canvas itself, a plane surface covered with colors, emotion

† Denis, *Théories, 1890–1910*, Paris, 1912, pp. 8–12. Translation by the editor.

[Decadence and Neo-Traditionalism]

arises, bitter or consoling, "literary" as painters say, without any need of interposing the reminder of some other sensation from past experience (like that of the motif from nature that is utilized). A Byzantine Christ is a symbol. The Jesus of modern painters, even if dressed in the most accurate turban, is only literary. In one, it is the form that is expressive; in the other it is an imitation of nature wishing to be so.

And just as I said that every kind of representation can be found in nature, so every beautiful work can excite the higher emotions, the self-contained ones, the ecstasy of the alexandrines. Even a simple experiment with lines * * * has an emotional value. Even the frieze of the Parthenon. Even, and above all, a great sonata by Beethoven!

There is only one true form of art. When you get rid of unjustifiable preconceived opinion and illogical prejudices, the field is left free for the painters' imagination, the esthetics of beautiful appearances. Neo-traditionalism [Denis himself, Vuillard, Bernard, Maillol] cannot be distracted by psychologies, whether scientific or fashionable, or by literary attachments that put down everything beyond their emotional range as myth. Neo-traditionalism attains definitive syntheses. Within the beauty of the work itself, everything coheres. * * * In this epoch of decadents who are, I hope, the primitives in this laborious preparation of something, those of us who lag behind are still the most finished.

Once more I look at the *Mona Lisa*. Oh, the voluptuousness of that blessed convention that displaces life, the artificial and exasperating life of a wax face that others seek! And the light! And the air! The blue arabesques of the background, the orange motif marvelously accompanying with a caressing and compelling rhythm, like the seduction of the violins in the *Tannhäuser* Overture!

MAURICE EMMANUEL

~~~~~~~

[*Notes on Debussy's Conversations
with Ernest Guiraud, 1890*]†

The following record of the conversations between Debussy and Ernest Guiraud was made by Maurice Emmanuel under curious circumstances. Whilst still a student at the Conservatoire, Emmanuel was attracted to the medieval modes and planned to introduce them in his compositions. This met with the stern disapproval of his master Léo Delibes, with the result that Emmanuel sought the support of the more broad-minded Guiraud with whom he was able to pursue his studies unofficially. Debussy had maintained a friendly relationship with his former master Guiraud, and in 1889 and 1890, after his visits to Bayreuth, often discussed aesthetic problems with him. These discussions were inspiring to Emmanuel to the extent that he jotted down some of the main points. Though they are set out in a haphazard fashion they light up a corner of the mind of Debussy at a time when Wagner was still a revolutionary and when the young Debussy was beginning to discover his way.   [Edward Lockspeiser]

GUIRAUD: You say that the cor anglais solo in the third act of *Tristan* is a classical aria, an 'exercise'? It doesn't in any way suggest Beethoven.

DEBUSSY: Because you don't hear the harmony beneath it. But let us look further. Berlioz is much further removed from Bach and Mozart than Wagner. He is less tonal than Wagner, though Wagner is more accomplished in transitions from major to minor.

GUIRAUD: How harsh; it's constantly chromatic. You can't call that classical.

DEBUSSY: Classical signifies major and minor.

In the classical, chords are resolved. The classical style implies near modulations (a closed circle).

† Reprinted from Edward Lockspeiser, *Debussy: His Life and Mind*, London, 1962, pp. 204–08. Reprinted with permission of The Macmillan Company. Published in the United States by The Macmillan Company, 1962. Reprinted by permission of Cassell & Co. Ltd.

[*Conversations, 1890*]

Romantic: a label that to my mind has no significance. The language of Schumann, Berlioz, and Liszt is the classical language. I hear in them all the same kind of music.

GUIRAUD: But this insipid, continuous music. No scenes, no cuts. You can't say it is anything like Mozart!

DEBUSSY: I shouldn't say it is the opposite of Mozart. It's a later development. No square-cut phrases, nevertheless Wagner develops in the classical manner. Wagner merely abandoned the perpetual perfect cadence and the hateful six-four chord. Supposing Mozart had had the idea of writing an act in one continuous movement, do you think he would have been able to achieve it? His was the convention of separate arias and four-bar phrases. Wagner develops in the classical manner. In the place of the architectural themes of a symphony, occurring at specified points, he has themes representing things and people, but he develops these themes in a symphonic manner. He derives from Bach and Beethoven, as we see in *Tristan* and *Meistersinger*—not to speak of his orchestra which is a development and enlargement of the classical orchestra.

GUIRAUD: But what about his treatment of the voices?

DEBUSSY: Yes, there we find a difference, but not a musical difference. Is it new? It may seem to resemble the spoken language; and it doesn't follow the four-bar phrase. There are no recitatives in the Italian manner and no lyrical arias. The words are subordinated to the orchestral accompaniment, but not sufficiently. It is music that sings too continuously. Singing should be reserved for certain points.

GUIRAUD: What kind of poet would you yourself have in mind?

DEBUSSY: One who only hints at what is to be said (*celui des choses dites à demi*). The ideal would be two associated dreams. No place, nor time. No big scene. No compulsion on the musician, who must complete and give body to the work of the poet. Music in opera is far too predominant. Too much singing and the musical settings are too cumbersome. The blossoming of the voice into true singing should occur only when required. A painting executed in grey is the ideal. No developments merely for the sake of developments. A prolonged development does not fit, cannot fit, the words. My idea is of a short libretto with mobile scenes. I have no use at all for the three unities. A variety of scenes in regard to place and character. No discussion or arguments between the characters whom I see at the mercy of life or destiny.

THE DIVISION OF THE OCTAVE
(Debussy seated at the piano)

DEBUSSY: 24 semitones=36 tones [1] in the octave with 18 different degrees. No faith in the supremacy of the C major scale. The tonal scale must be enriched by other scales.

I am not misled by equal temperament. Rhythms are stifling. Rhythms cannot be contained within bars. It is nonsense to speak of 'simple' and 'composed' time. There should be an interminable flow of them both without seeking to bury the rhythmic patterns. Relative keys are nonsense too. Music is neither major nor minor. Minor thirds and major thirds should be combined, modulation thus becoming more flexible. The mode is that which one happens to choose at the moment. It is inconstant. In *Tristan* the themes heard in the orchestra are themes of the action. They do no violence to the action. There must be a balance between musical demands and thematic evocation. Themes suggest their orchestral colouring.

GUIRAUD *(Debussy having played a series of intervals on the piano)*: What's that?

DEBUSSY: Incomplete chords, floating. *Il faut noyer le ton.* One can travel where one wishes and leave by any door. Greater nuances.

GUIRAUD: But when I play this it has to resolve.

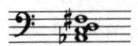

DEBUSSY: I don't see that it should. Why?
GUIRAUD: Well, do you find this lovely?

1. "Trente six" might perhaps mean merely "dozens" or "lots." [*Editor*]

[*Conversations, 1890*]

DEBUSSY: Yes, yes, yes!
GUIRAUD: But how would you get out of this.

I am not saying that what you do isn't beautiful, but it's theoretically absurd.
DEBUSSY: There is no theory. You have merely to listen. Pleasure is the law.
GUIRAUD: I would agree with you in regard to an exceptional person who has discovered a discipline for himself and who has an instinct which he is able to impose. But how would you teach music to others?
DEBUSSY: Music cannot be learnt.
GUIRAUD: Come now, you are forgetting that you yourself were ten years at the Conservatoire.
DEBUSSY: (*He agrees to this and admits that there can nevertheless be a doctrine*): Yes, this is silly. Except that I can't reconcile all this. True enough, I feel free because I have been through the mill, and I don't write in the fugal style because I know it. (*He is astonishingly direct in discussion and never seeks to avoid a point with a joke.*)

* * *

CLAUDE DEBUSSY

[Letters to Ernest Chausson]†

Ernest Chausson (1855-99) left the Conservatory as soon as he entered it in 1880, preferring to study with César Franck for the next three years. So he probably did not meet Debussy until the end of the '80s. By then he had composed his symphony in B♭, Op. 20, and was working on an opera, *King Arthur*. His most famous work, the *Poème* for violin and orchestra, Op. 25, was finished in 1896. Debussy's letters to Chausson are unique in their ample discussion of critical questions that concerned the two friends throughout the '90s.

Saturday 26 August 1893

Dear friend,
 Claude Achille had to put off the pleasure of writing to you the past several days because of a bad fever that kept me in bed—dismal, stupefied. It made my fingers run over the covers like rabbits. It all began with a sad evening when, after having said good-bye to you, Bonheur and I wandered off together, unable to drag out of ourselves anything but little phrases whose monotony drove us to despair; when I got home I was completely demoralized and our leaving seemed to me definitely an irreparable accident. * * *
 As for your sermons, they will always be very mild to me; aren't you a little like a big elder brother in whom one has complete faith, from whom one would accept even scoldings? Pardon me if up to now I have not been able to succeed in satisfying you, but be assured that your reproaches will be such a punishment to me that I cannot help making

† From *Revue musicale*, VII/1 (Nov. 1925), 117–26. Translation by the editor. Reprinted by permission of La Revue Musicale.

every effort not to deserve them.

I feel as you do the absolute usefulness of effort, but when it is besmirched by the trivialities of existence it sometimes become depressing, especially when you see how little interest it arouses in people who easily change effort into "technique." If you want to protect from such mud-splashings the ideal or illusion of the thing for which we suffer—that is, art—this becomes appalling. For people pretend not to be bothered by questions that interest them only artificially, and I am still speaking of only a small number! The artist, in modern civilizations, will always be a being whose usefulness is acknowledged only after his death, and then only to take a stupid pride in it, or to gamble on it, always shamefully. Hence it would be better for him never to mingle with his contemporaries. Indeed what's the use of having them participate, by any sort of performance, in those joys for whom so few are fit! It will be enough if you are "discovered" much later, for certain recent glories will surely have terrible responsibilities to assume as to the future.

Now, dear friend, let me embrace you with all my heart and ask you to give all my greetings to Mme. Chausson, Anny, Etiennette, Marianne, Jean, Sébastien, Michel.

Yours,
Claude Debussy.

Sunday (6 September 1893)

Dear friend,

It's no use, I can't succeed in laughing off the sadness of my landscape. Sometimes my days are dark and silent, like those of a hero of Edgar Allen Poe, and my soul as romantic as a ballade of Chopin! My solitude is populated with too many memories which I cannot get rid of. Well, one must live and wait! It remains to be seen whether I haven't a bad ticket for Bonheur's omnibus; however, I shall be content with a place on the upper deck. (Excuse this bargain philosophy!)

So the hour has chimed for my thirty-first year, and I am not yet very sure of my esthetic, and there are things I still don't know! (how to make masterpieces, for instance; then how to be very serious, among other things, for I have the fault of dreaming my life too much and not seeing the realities until the moment when they are becoming insuperable.) Perhaps I am more to be pitied than condemned. In any case, writing you this, I count on your pardon, and your patience.

I had a visit from Henri de Régnier. He displays a great sympathy for you. That is like talking about a rope in the home of a hanged man! Also, with no reward, I brought out my best Sunday behavior and played *L'Après-midi d'un faune,* whose heat he finds like an oven, and whose shivering he praises! (Fit that together as you may.) But when he talks poetry he becomes deeply interesting and shows a quite sharp sensitivity.

As he was telling me of certain words in the French language whose gold was tarnished by too much use in the rude world, I thought to myself that the same is true for certain chords whose sound has become banal in commercial music. This reflection is not thrillingly novel, unless I add that the chords have at the same time lost their symbolic essence.

Truly, music should have been a secret science, preserved by texts whose interpretation was so long and hard that it would surely have discouraged the crowd of people who make use of it as casually as one uses a pocket handkerchief. Now, *and further,* instead of trying to diffuse art in the public, I propose the establishment of a "Society of Musical Esotericism," and you will see that M. Helmann won't be there, nor will M. de Bonnières!

While I have been writing you, a girl at the piano on the floor below me has been sawing on music in D which is terrifying! and this is a living proof, alas!, that I am all too right.

And you, dear friend, do lots of work, be peaceful, don't have any more pretty little children to make a racket like half a million thunders! Have you definitely killed off the poor Genièvre [heroine of Chausson's opera]? The last thing you showed me made me anticipate excessively beautiful music from you! In any case I wait for you confidently. I myself am slogging away but, whether it is the misanthropy of my life or what, I am not happy with what I do. I wish you were here a little, I am afraid of working in the void, then that takes on the fascinations of a young savage which I cannot resist.

Oh, your poor Claude Achille waits like another Sister Anne for your return, which will restore joy to his heart, and he embraces you affectionately.

Claude Debussy.

P.S. I have just finished the last *Prose lyrique,* dedicated to H. Lerolle, first because it gives me pleasure and then so as not to drop out of a cycle of friendship.

Received a letter from V. d'Indy, quite friendly. Praises that would bring a blush to the lilies that slumber between the hands of the Blessed Damozel.

C. A. Debussy finishes a scene of *Pelléas and Mélisande,* "A fountain in the park" (Act IV, scene IV), for which he would like to have the advice of E. Chausson. One wonders whether there might not be a way of organizing the pleasure trains between Paris and Royan [Chausson's home] to facilitate this eventuality, whose great interest we need not further indicate.

Monday 2 October 1893

Dear friend,

My only excuse for having given you so many long days without a letter is that I have worked too much! You have been so good, anyway, as to have guessed that this could be the only reason. There is also, of course, a bit of weariness at writing you things that I would so much like to tell you! Yes, time hangs heavy on me, and the sadness of not seeing you has been growing for so many days—let me say it to you; please overlook the too frequent recurrence of the same complaints, and know that among the annoying things in my gray life it is still your absence that takes first place.

I was too hasty to crow over *Pelléas and Mélisande.* For, after sleeping on it, I had to admit to myself that it wasn't that at all. It was like the duo of M. Somebody, or Anybody, and above all the ghost of old Klingsor, alias R. Wagner, appeared at the turn of a measure, so I tore it all up and have begun again on the search for a little chemistry of more personal phrases. I have tried to be Pelléas as well as Mélisande. I have been looking for music behind all the veils that accumulate around it even for its most ardent devotees! I have brought back from the search something that you will perhaps like; as for others it is no matter to me. I have made use (quite spontaneously, moreover) of a means that seems to me rather rare, namely of silence (don't laugh) as an agent of expression and perhaps the only way of making effective the emotion of a phrase. For although Wagner used it, it seems to me it is only in a quite dramatic way. Rather like other ambiguous dramas in the style of Bouchardy, Ennery, and so on!

Oh, if times were less sad, if one could ask people to take an interest in anything but a new model of bicycle! But then I don't know why I say this for I have no intention whatever of ruling over the mind of my contemporaries. But all the same it would be nice to establish a school of neomusicians, in which one would try to preserve intact the marvelous symbols of music, in which one would at least restore respect for an art that so many others have soiled, and the crowd would learn to discriminate a bit in its enthusiasm and would distinguish a *Franck* from a Massenet, and his likes would be no more than poor actors. A few booths at the fair would be enough for the performance of their poor conceptions. Besides, we owe this state of things to the motto inscribed on our monuments: Liberty, Equality, Fraternity, which are words at most for cab drivers. * * *

Monday

* * * One thing that I should like to see you lose is the preoccupation with the "underpinnings." I'll explain: I believe that we have been taken in, always by the same R. Wagner, and that too often we think of the frame before having the picture, and that sometimes the richness of the frame makes us overlook the poverty of the idea—not to mention the case in which magnificent underpinnings clothe ideas comparable to ten-cent dolls! It would be better, it seems to me, to take the opposite side, that is, to find the perfect outline of an idea and then add to it only what ornament it requires, for truly "certain people" are like priests bedecking in priceless jewels their wooden idols! Look at the poverty of symbol hidden in several of the last sonnets of Mallarmé, where still the craft of the artisan is carried to its furthest limits, and look at Bach, where everything works together fantastically to make the idea effective, where the lightness of the underpinnings never absorbs the main point. But these are things familiar to you, and I say them only for the sake of conversation. * * *

Monday [early in 1894]

* * * Now I must say, too, that I have had some days of real grief

over what you told me about my quartet, for I have felt that after all it had only made you like *certain things* more, whereas I should have wanted it to make you forget them. Well, I shall make another that will be for you, and seriously for you, and I shall try to give my forms some nobility. I should like to have enough influence on you to be able to scold you and tell you you are mistaken about yourself! You exert so strong a pressure on your ideas that they no longer dare to come before you spontaneously, they are so afraid of not being clothed as would suit you. You don't let yourself go enough. And above all you don't seem to allow enough free play to that mysterious thing that enables us to find the right impression of a feeling, whereas surely a diligent, dogged search only weakens it. I am so sure that you have in you all the desirable expression that I hate to see you wear yourself out in useless arguments. Indeed, it must be said that we are nothing at all in the face of art; we are only the instrument of a destiny; therefore we must let it fulfill itself! Perhaps I have no right to speak to you in this way, but pardon me and recognize in it above all only my great wish to see you as you ought to be, and that as lofty as possible, because you can do it better than anyone. Also take of this only what you want; you know well enough that I don't mean to give you advice!! but I should merely like to give you courage to believe in yourself.

Will you be at Brussels up to the first of March to hear the Debussy Festival? * * *

RAYMOND BONHEUR

[*The "First Stage" of the* Faun]†

Raymond Bonheur (1851–1939) was a friend and fellow-student of Debussy's, who shared his literary tastes, unusual at the Conservatory. After the *Faun*, which was dedicated to Bonheur, Debussy seems to have lost

† From Bonheur's memoir in *Revue musicale*, VII (1926), 102. Translation by the editor. Reprinted by permission of La Revue Musicale.

touch with his old friend, whose name is now remembered almost exclusively for his six pages of recollections, published after Debussy's death.

It was when he played from a still-fluid sketch, almost in the fever of inspiration, that he was truly prodigious. "How I envy the painters," he said, "who can keep the freshness of the sketch as they dream it." I shall always remember the dazzled sensation I experienced when he showed me, in its first stage, that *Après-midi d'un faune,* streaming with light, blazing with all the ardors of summer, whose blinding flash, however, took a long time to overcome certain false claims. It was on a radiant afternoon (he then lived on the Rue de Londres * * *), and beside the big open window, the setting sun came clear through to the back of the room. * * * This *Après-midi d'un faune,* I have often heard it since, but no performance, however perfect, has made me forget those moments.

GUSTAVE DORET

[*The First Performance of the* Faun]†

The Swiss composer and conductor Gustave Doret (1866–1943) came to Paris in 1892 after studying in Berlin. His account of conducting the première of the *Faun* was doubtless retold many times before he published it in his memoirs, just a year before he died.

The Société Nationale could admit no principles other than those of d'Indy. * * * The public, if not also the rather few members of the group themselves, had gradually abandoned its concerts. The committee had determined that the society should be awakened from this quasi-somnolence. They hired the Salle d'Harcourt and its orchestra. They called me. At once I grasped the difficulties of a delicate and com-

† From Doret's *Temps et contretemps,* Fribourg, 1942, pp. 94 ff. Translation by the editor. Reprinted by permission of R. de Wuilleret.

plex situation, but for me the honor was great. Unanimously the general meeting elected me (though a foreigner) a member of the committee and designated me conductor of the concerts. The first concert that I was to conduct was set for December 23, 1894, and as I anticipated, I was to undergo a serious test.

C. A. Debussy was going to entrust me, at this debut of mine, with the first performance of the *Prélude à "L'Après-midi d'un faune."* He took me to his little apartment on Rue Gustave Doré (funny coincidence!), spread out the proofs of the orchestral score, already covered with corrections, and sat down at the piano; meanwhile, with mouth gaping and ears strained I sat beside him.

Anyone who has never heard Debussy himself play his works at the piano in private cannot quite do justice to the Debussyesque art, an art so incorporeal, so subtle that only the author, with his extraordinary hands guided by his profound sensibility, could give it its perfect interpretation.

What force, then, did the violent accents take under his fist! By what extraordinary gifts was he able at the keyboard to give his score the colors of his orchestra, with the most perfect balance, even in the instrumental nuances?

The hour of this revelation of the famous *Prelude* I shall never forget. I was completely seduced, ravished, captured, what shall I say? And Claude Achille, finding in me an echo, sincere and accurate, played his score over several times for my greater joy. Together we envisaged the very great difficulties of a perfect performance. For try to understand what a revolution Debussy brought into the technique of instrumentation! What to any conductor today seems only a simple formula, in those times raised problems that had to be solved, so much so that Debussy had great misgivings, doubtful himself about certain effects that he hoped to obtain. I assured him that we would take all the time needed for this delicate preparation. All the same, I believe that there never was a more intimate collaboration than that which we shared in the working sessions. Gradually the musicians of the orchestra, excellent as ever, became eager to express completely the Debussyesque thought. Constantly Debussy modified this or that sonority. We tried; we started over; then we compared. Everyone kept calm: patience should be the watchword without which no good work can be accomplished. The piece had reached its definitive form. The players, having gotten used to this new style, understood that we would have to fight a serious battle. Of course

Debussy was not unknown to the true connoisseurs, but the big public was still ignorant of him. Would it try to resist? We wondered all the more since, for this first concert, I had arranged that the hall be full and that the work not be played only for the usual limited circle of the Société Nationale.

Debussy had written his masterpiece; the players and I had satisfied him, translating his thought, he said, as he had never hoped; "to perfection" he kept exclaiming at the last rehearsal.

But the hour of the great test has arrived. Debussy hides his anxiety with a grin that I well knew. He presses my hands. The orchestra tunes up in the corridor. I ask for silence. "My friends," I say to the musicians, "you know that we are going to defend a great cause this evening. If you have some friendship for Debussy and for me, you will give yourselves completely." My good colleagues applauded: "Don't worry, maestro! we'll win."

I ascend the podium with some emotion, but much reassured and full of confidence. I wait a long moment after having imposed silence on the last lingering conversations among the audience. The hall is packed. An impressive silence reigns, when our marvelous flutist Barrère unrolls his opening theme. * * *

Suddenly I feel behind my back—it is a special ability of certain conductors—a completely captivated public! The triumph is complete, so much so that in spite of the rule forbidding encores I did not hesitate to break the rule. The orchestra, delighted, joyfully repeated the work that it had loved and had imposed on the conquered public. * * *

Imagine the welcome that Debussy was saving for me in the corridor when I came down from the podium. From that time our friendship was more solidly established than ever. I may add that until his death he testified the most loyal gratitude to me, while I felt greatly indebted to him for the trust he had put in me in such serious circumstances.

PIERRE LOUŸS

[*Letter to Debussy, December 23, 1894*]†

Pierre Louÿs (1870–1925) launched his career as poet in 1891 by founding a review, *La Conque,* to which his friends Régnier, Gide, and Valéry contributed. All these young disciples of Mallarmé knew Debussy. Louÿs became his most intimate friend for several years, and doubtless his chief literary mentor. Among the main works of Louÿs are his erotic *Chansons de Bilitis* (1894), from which Debussy chose a few for songs (1898).

My dear Debussy,

Your *Prelude* is admirable. I want to tell you so at once, the moment I come home. It was not possible to make a more delicious paraphrase of the verses that we both love. There is always a breeze in the leaves, and so varied, so changing.

I owe you a real joy: not the first one, you know.

I shall see you tomorrow, no doubt at Lamoureux, because I surely will not go to Harcourt.

To hear your piece again I shall wait for a slightly better performance. The horns stank, and the rest were hardly better.

Yours,
PL

† Louÿs, *Neuf lettres à Debussy* (1894–98), in *Revue de musicologie,* XLVIII (1962), 62. Translation by the editor. Reprinted by permission of Librairie José Corti.

FRANCIS GRIERSON

~~~~~~~~

[*The Circle Is Now Complete, 1913*]†

The other night, at Covent Garden, we saw the incomparable Nijinsky mimic the Faun in Stéphane Mallarmé's delightful poem, with music by Debussy. When, years ago, I had those memorable talks with the poet, I little thought the day would come when *The Afternoon of a Faun* would receive a baptism of inspired music at the hands of the most gifted musician of his kind, and a stage portrayal by the greatest choreographic artist living.

The performance at Covent Garden was a triumph for three—the poet, the composer, and the dancer. The circle is now complete.

Stéphane Mallarmé is now almost popular, and popularity is what he most dreaded.

* * * Many of the young visitors to Mallarmé's salon are now celebrities. * * *

---

† Grierson, "Stéphane Mallarmé," *Poetry*, II (Apr.–Sep. 1913), 104–07. Reprinted by permission of *Poetry*.

CRITICISM AND ANALYSIS

As in the preceding section, here too the student may find a selection from a vast literature, including the chief discussions that are cited in the introduction. Further readings are suggested in the bibliography. Unless otherwise specified, all numbered footnotes in the following essays are those of the author.

ALFRED BRUNEAU

[*Seeking the Exceptional*]†

Alfred Bruneau (1857–1934) wrote his most famous opera, *Le Rêve* (1887), and several others on librettos drawn from the works of Émile Zola. His critical journalism makes evident his up-to-date musical craftsmanship and his independence of mind.

I was happy to see the announcement of an unpublished piece on the poster for the first concert of this season.

MM. Colonne and Lamoureux, who are popularizing the glorious names of Berlioz and Wagner by an equal insistence in repeating the same programs, have finally grasped the need of renewing their repertory. At the Châtelet we are promised for every Sunday a work by a young French musician. At the Summer Circus we are to hear the great oratorios of Bach and Handel. At the opera, too, we shall have important compositions old and new. Here are noble projects worthy of unreserved approval.

Since victory, complete and definitive, has marked the end of the ardent battles waged for Wagner and Berlioz, I should wish very much that now there might begin, with resolution and courage, the fight for our national school, which has no other battleground than the concert hall. If Pasdeloup had not long ago led his campaign in just this direction, very few of our current masters of the theater could have won their places. Today it is said there is a famine of dramatic musicians. You can find the cause for that in the fact that for several years our conductors—with the most laudable aim of artistic propaganda, to be sure—have stayed too faithfully with the "repertory."

So endless gratitude is due M. Colonne for reacting against this situation. His courage is further attested by the choice of the new work

† *Figaro*, October 14, 1895, p. 3. Translation by the editor.

that he has just let us hear.

The author of this work, M. Claude Debussy, is still unknown to the public. Up till now it has had no chance to get acquainted with his compositions, altogether curious and original, among which I should cite at least a string quartet of a very free rhythmic fantasy, and some songs on poems of Baudelaire and Verlaine that attain a quite amazing intensity of expression.

M. Debussy, legitimately abhorring the trite and banal, and increasingly—to my slight regret—seeking the exceptional, has now undertaken to explain to us symphonically the eclogue of M. Stéphane Mallarmé, *L'Après-midi d'un faune.* An arduous task! For this eclogue, whose peculiar spell, cast by the vague combinations of syllables and subtle associations of tones, I should never deny, is very hermetic, as they say. It is an almost purely musical poem, this one of M. Mallarmé, and the task of M. Debussy consisted in somehow translating it into the language of instruments, seizing on the wing its fleeting sonorities and fixing them with the aid of a traditional notation.

I am afraid that last night's public, though responding warmly, did not altogether understand these things. It could not penetrate, I fear, the mists of dream where there sing, under the imprecise harmonies of the violins and harps, the pastoral flutes, the rustic oboes, and where there resound the mysterious horns. This is a great pity, for the work has its moments of truly exquisite music, and, if candor obliges me to confess a preference for an art more neat, more robust, more masculine, yet justice compels me to recognize that M. Debussy has a rare and original temperament. M. Colonne must be complimented for having let us hear this curious fantasy and for having played it with the necessary care for nuances, tempi, and rhythms.

Meanwhile, the master violinist Sarasate played superbly Lalo's *Symphonie espagnole,* a pure marvel of wit, grace, and verve, which recalls in its orchestral flowering the adorable *Namouna.* Mme. Marx-Goldschmitt won sustained applause with the fine C-minor concerto of M. Saint-Saëns, so well-built, so clearly organized, so noble and firm in its simplicity.

GUSTAVE ROBERT

[*A Style of His Own, 1895*]†

Though the author of this review was an obscure journalist, his allegation about the resemblance of Debussy's "middle" theme to Massenet has been repeated by many writers. His worries about tonality, together with his neglect of rhythm and sound, likewise became commonplace, often without as much study of the score as Robert must have done.

The Colonne concerts are really looking interesting. * * * The most striking novelty is to have included in the program at the very start of the season the work of a young author, the *Prélude à "L'Après-midi d'un faune"* of M. Debussy. * * *

The piece of M. Debussy, although written as a prelude to the poem of Mallarmé, cannot be considered as a descriptive work. It has a somewhat personal character, and that is all. But from the musical point of view, if we take it as an example of the rather special genre that M. Debussy has created, it is really interesting.

M. Debussy's music presents this peculiarity: it is almost outside of all tonality. And this absence of tonality is obtained by the use of the following procedures.

The use—it isn't enough to say just that. These procedures are known and practiced by all musicians. M. Debussy's peculiarity is to make constant use of them. And it is doubtless on this point that he has rather exposed himself to the critics. However good something may be, it should not be used beyond all reason. Not to mention the fatigue for the ear that results from this constantly fleeting tonality, it is certain that a fine chord is considerably weakened if it is lost and as if drowned amid the waves of dissonances.

† *Revue illustré*, XX/228, 229 (November 1 and 15, 1895), 2 and 1. Translation by the editor.

One of M. Debussy's procedures consists in ignoring altogether the key indicated in the signature and in changing the key at every repetition of the motif. Thus in the *Prelude,* without speaking of the exposition of the theme which is not harmonized at all but which is notated as in E major, as soon as the motif recurs we are in D major. Then we pass to E. The third time we are still in E but with another position of the chord. From here we modulate to A, and so on to the end. It must be noted, however, that this piece ends on the tonic chord of the key.

Another procedure: almost always in the motif itself, and to the same extent, it is remarkable that modulations are most often to very remote keys. Thus at the beginning of the third of the *Proses lyriques* we find a succession of five common chords: C, B♭ minor, G, B♭ minor, and finally C.

Again, it is remarkable that hardly ever does a chord appear with emphasis in its natural position. Almost always M. Debussy introduces a foreign note. Likewise he almost always alters one of the scale degrees. * * *

Finally, another procedure of M. Debussy is to use certain diatonic lines that give a scale with a quite peculiar effect. I shall cite as examples the *Proses lyriques* (p. 4, at the syllables *meuse*), the ascending scale in the right hand; and again the *Prelude,* p. 6 of the reduction for two pianos, line 2, the ascending passage that goes by steps from F to E♯.

Surely the procedure is among the most debatable. Still it must be acknowledged that in certain cases it can give quite pretty effects. Thus I think that it lends to the pastoral theme of the *Prelude* its peculiar savor. Doubtless the line goes by chromatic steps, but it is remarkable that from the C♯ to the G there is precisely the interval of four steps.

Our accepting this motif, from which so many others are wrenched out, does not mean that we fully subscribe to M. Debussy's piece. We must not omit to say that we find the motif a bit drowned in the harmonies and rhythms with which the author surrounds it. Thus surely when it is exposed in 12/8 meter, the harp arpeggios that last through two beats are rather calculated to throw off the listener. We shall say also that the interlude of the middle section seems to us not to be of equal originality. Perhaps we will seem hard to please, but leave out the chords and there remains a phrase that is not unlike the manner of M. Massenet. To people fond of such rather pedantic comparisons I shall recall the phrase of the piece called "The Virgin's Last Sleep."

But with these reservations we must acknowledge all the skill and all the care M. Debussy has shown in his *Prelude*. Doubtless the development is not quite what we should have hoped. Sometimes it seems that there is repetition with changed chords rather than true development. But it must be granted that as a whole the piece is truly tightly woven. Aside from the episode in the middle (which is reasonable *qua* episode) and the four measures in 3/4 found on pp. 6 and 7 of the piano reduction, there is nothing not derived from the motif itself.

Altogether M. Debussy has the great merit of having created a style of his own. It is a very simple, perhaps very sincere, manner, and of the best coinage, so that we may get used to it very gladly. Perhaps there is even more merit in being original with simplicity than in being original in complexity. But whatever path they follow, we should pay tribute to all innovators without discrimination, and M. Debussy is doubtless among these.

CAMILLE SAINT-SAËNS

[*Letter to Maurice Emmanuel*]†

Camille Saint-Saëns (1835–1921) was prodigious from childhood on into his eighties. When Debussy's career began, Saint-Saëns was enjoying the fame of his Third Symphony and his *Carnival of Animals* (both 1886). His opera *Samson et Dalila,* performed first in Weimar in 1877, reached Paris at last in 1892. Debussy had loved the score since 1883. By the time of *Pelléas,* Saint-Saëns's generally adverse judgment of Debussy was well known, but it was only in 1920, after Debussy's death, that he wrote a comment on the *Faun* in particular.

Dear Sir,

Your very interesting lecture on Debussy has come to my attention; since its elegant and attractive form has captivated me, will you allow me to tell you that basically I do not share your opinion? I should not

† *Revue musicale,* 206 (1947), 30–31. Translation by the editor. Reprinted by permission of La Revue Musicale.

dare to say so publicly: I should appear to harbor ill feelings that are far from my mind.

"You are happy," a great composer said to me once. "You are not jealous!" "My goodness," I replied to him, "jealously is an act of humility that I am not capable of."

Jealousy is so common a disease that it cannot fail to be attributed to me. But for your sole benefit, why shouldn't I say what I think?

Ah! Claude Debussy was lucky! The public did not yet know a note of his when the Press began to sing his praises; review articles even proclaimed his genius; then the works succeeded with the public; it was prepared. * * *

The need for novelty at any cost is a disease of our time. Formerly in all the arts, even arts and crafts, all artists used the same formulæ, which did not prevent the first-class ones from asserting their personality; to do so they had only to trust their *natural* gifts, for when a person has any he is necessarily original without being aware of it, and when a person has none the search for originality leads only to the Baroque, to daubing, to noise. It is true that "by familiarity combinations of sound that at first were intolerably harsh are finally welcomed with favor." Yes, it is true that one gets accustomed to everything—to dirt, even to crime; but there are simply some things that one must not get used to. Familiarity has already gone too far; the public has supported *Salome,* and now it is applauding a work where trumpets violently fill your ears with successions of fourths and fifths. It is a return to the first efforts in Harmony; it is not music any longer. The extremes meet.

What annoys me most about Debussy is his "putting on," and the naïveté with which the public is taken in by it.

He announces "Gardens in the Rain," attractive title that recalls the "Wet Woods" of Victor Hugo; and he gives us an endless series of arpeggios on "Sleep, Baby, Sleep" and "We Won't Go to the Woods Anymore."

He announces the "Dialogue of the Wind and the Wave" and you hear a trumpet playing "Here's Your Fun, My Ladies."

The *Prélude à "L'Après-midi d'un faune"* is pretty sound, but you find in it not the slightest musical idea properly speaking. It is as much like a piece of music as the palette a painter has worked with is like a painting.

In *Pelléas,* where he has suppressed not only singing but declamation, except for the final scene, the music is not at all appropriate for the play; it could just as well fit anything else.

Debussy has not created a style: he has cultivated the absence of style, of logic, and of common sense.

But he had a euphonious name. If he had been called Martin he would never have been talked about. In this case it is true that he would probably have adopted a pseudonym. * * *

PAUL DUKAS

[Reviews of Debussy's Music]†

Paul Dukas (1865–1935) composed his most famous work, the symphonic poem based on Goethe's *Sorcerer's Apprentice*, in 1897. A friend of Debussy's, though not a close one, Dukas received as a gift from him in 1887 a copy of Mallarmé's *Faun*, just published in its definitive edition. Dukas followed Debussy's whole career with sympathy and thorough understanding. He became a highly respected teacher at the Conservatory, passing on the best of traditional craft and taste to many pupils, including Olivier Messiaen. Dukas's critical writings, not voluminous, are all worth reading. (Debussy wrote to Dukas, January 11, 1894, ". . . how much I value your criticisms." This letter was exhibited at the Bibliothèque Nationale, and is cited in the exhibition catalogue, *Paul Dukas*, Paris, 1965, p. 6.)

Dukas surpassed all these appreciations of Debussy after his friend's death, by writing a piano piece "Plainte du faune," on motifs of the *Prelude*. This was published along with compositions of Satie, Bartók, Stravinsky, Schmitt, Falla, and Malipiero, in the special issue of the *Revue musicale* devoted to Debussy, 1920.

DEBUSSY'S QUARTET
(May, 1894)

The evening of chamber music recently given by M. de Guarnieri, with the collaboration of MM. Henri Falk, Lammers, Ruffin, and Rerriou,

† Originally published in *L'Hebdomadaire*, these reviews are reprinted in the collection of Dukas's *Écrits*, Paris, 1948, pp. 173, 529, 600. Translation by the editor. Reprinted by permission of Editions SEFI, Paris.

was among the most interesting of the season. Besides the quintet of César Franck—a classic already—and a sonata for cello and piano by M. Edvard Grieg, there was heard a quartet by M. C. A. Debussy; among recent productions in this genre, it is certainly one of the most worthy to hold the attention of connoisseurs. This was not the first time that we heard this quartet. The great violinist Eugène Ysaÿe had already played it at a brilliant concert of the Société Nationale. At that time we had been able to enjoy fully the harmonious daring and the exquisite refinements of M. Debussy's work. The concert of the Guarnieri quartet, now reviving the impressions that we had gathered from this transcendant performance, has allowed us to define them still better.

What we have written elsewhere about the symphony in general may be applied as well to the quartet and to every sort of pure music. The dramatic tendencies of music since Beethoven are undeniable, to be sure; but, we repeat once more, it would be excessively pedantic, in the face of a strong work or only a charming work of a distinctive artist, to maintain the theoretical point of view that was held by Wagner (who held it, moreover, because of his own temperament and the needs of his cause) and to repeat more or less blindly what he had promulgated only to support his conviction as music-dramatist. Whatever may be said, or thought, or written, there will always be some artists more exclusively musicians than others. It must be granted that if one of these artists, spontaneously and by virtue of an urge that has nothing to do with any symphonic idea, writes an original work, it is absurd as well as narrow-minded to condemn him in the name of an abstract principle. By the very *existence* of a work that it forbids, this principle stands confirmed.

M. Debussy, one of the most richly gifted and most original of the new musical generation, belongs undeniably to this class of composers who see in music not the means but the end, and who consider it less as an instrument of expression than as the expression itself. He is a lyricist, in the full meaning of the term. If he sets a given text, he tries not so much to put his thought at its service as to record, by a sort of personal paraphrase, the musical impressions suggested to him by reading the poem. Given this peculiar sort of mind, one may imagine that in spite of the opera-composer's education inflicted uniformly on all competitors for the Prix de Rome at the Conservatory where he studied, M. Debussy, after having composed several volumes of beautiful and tasteful songs, and a very distinctive setting of Dante Gabriel

Rosetti's *Blessed Damozel* for soloists, chorus, and orchestra, should quite naturally have come to pure music.

A fantasy in three movements for piano and orchestra and the quartet we are about to discuss are the first results of this new direction of ideas.

M. Debussy's quartet is a work in which the intensity of color might at first seem to predominate over the expression proper. But this is only how it seems. By the very definition we have given of M. Debussy's temperament, he proposes to characterize nothing but musical feelings, contrary to what may be observed among many composers for whom music is only a more vehement way of rendering general impressions and thought. A superficial listener might even be led to think that M. Debussy's music means nothing. In this he would be very mistaken. For, if the quartet in question contains none of those incisive accents, nor those periods of almost dramatic development so frequent among other composers (justified by Wagner's theory), if the sense of M. Debussy's work is absolutely musical, does this mean that it is deprived of sense? Yes, if one allows that expression is the monopoly belonging exclusively to tremolos and diminished sevenths. No, if one believes on the contrary that instrumental music contains its intrinsic goal and that, rather than trying to deck out a more or less foreign meaning, it should move us without ever leaving its own field of action. This opinion, it is known, was held by Mozart. For him music should always remain music, no matter what it might propose to express. Recently the Russian school has appealed to the same principle. M. Debussy seems to us, even though our assertion may strike him as a paradox, to belong in this respect to the school of Mozart. He adheres to it as do Weber, Chopin, Schumann, and in general all the masters who have shown a sort of horror for the far-fetched dramatization of music, and to the same degree. The line of Beethoven is quite different. It includes especially composers who have shown a contrary tendency, a sort of discomfort in the fact of pure music without precise meaning, and who have always tried to fix the meaning of the symphonic works that they admired. Such were Berlioz and Wagner.

The quartet of M. Debussy clearly shows the stamp of his manner. Everything in it is clear and clearly drawn, despite a great liberty of form. The melodic essence of the work is concentrated but rich in flavor. It is enough to fill the harmonic texture with a penetrating and original poetry. The harmony itself, in spite of great boldness, is never jarring or harsh. M. Debussy likes in particular successions of thick chords, with dissonant intervals, never raw, rather more harmonious in their complication than the consonant intervals themselves. His melody proceeds over the chords as if over a sumptuous carpet, ingeniously ornate with strange colors from which all shrill and conflicting tones had been ruled out.

A single theme serves as the basis of all the movements of the work. Some of its transformations are particularly captivating in their unexpected grace. Thus for example the one that is found in the middle section of the scherzo (this movement is only an ingenious variation of the motive). Nothing could be more charming than the expressive return of the rhythmic theme, accompanied by the light quivering of crossing strings in the second violin and viola, and by the plucked notes of the cello. If it were necessary to avow our preference among the four movements, we should choose the first and the andante—truly exquisitely poetic and supremely delicate in thought.

M. de Guarnieri and his colleagues played M. Debussy's work with great care for the detail and an artistic conviction worthy of all praise.

DEBUSSY'S NOCTURNES
(February, 1901)

M. Debussy holds a unique place among today's musicians. Critics and public, both fond of classifying when they encounter a new manifestation of this strange and delicate talent, hardly know what to think, and they let it be seen easily enough. M. Debussy cannot be ranked in any of the categories in which contemporary composers are conveniently listed: pupils of Franck, pupils of Massenet, disciples of Wagner, devotees of Liszt, etc., each one has its anthropometrical label in the police lineup of current opinion. M. Debussy has none. It is known that he was the pupil of good old Guiraud at the Conservatory, but this hardly contributes to making his pedigree precise. His music is so little like that of [Guiraud's] *Carnaval* or *Piccolino*! Further, M. Debussy himself seems to enjoy disconcerting his admirers—for he has some very ardent ones; none of his works seems to be what was expected to follow the one before; all of them have something unique, which indicates, if not a very perceptible change of his manner, at least a different and unexpected point of view.

These sudden changes of horizon are reflected in his work in various, often opposed, colorations, whose alternations are apt to disturb the judgment of the whole that one might be tempted to form of it. Thus, for example, nothing is less like *L'Après-midi d'un faune* than the *Nocturnes,* of which M. Chevillard has just acquainted us with two movements. The external procedures, no doubt, scarcely differ from one composition to the other; the musical language remains approximately the same: the search for the most subtle harmonies again forms almost all the structures and the composer shows his preoccupation, as before, with fixing the dominant character of his work by the notation of a series of sensations rather than the deductions of a musical thought directly related to the poetic expression. But if the tone of the discourse remains perceptibly the same, its object is entirely different: this is enough to change its aspect, to modify the angle from which its sense is communicated to us.

Thus each work of M. Debussy brings us a new surprise, which is the explanation of the difficulty in classifying him experienced by those who like to be informed, once and for all, of an artist's tendencies. The fact is, M. Debussy is unclassifiable.

It is not impossible, however, to specify the essential traits of a production already extensive and so diverse. Independent of the characteristics we have just assigned him, one can point out others that allow us to grasp the nature of this production. The choice of poetic themes that M. Debussy adopts as pretext for his musical fantasy—this in itself is a precious index. Whether he collaborates with Baudelaire, Verlaine, or Mallarmé, or draws from his own resources the subject of his works, the composer shows above all his concern to avoid what might be called the direct translation of feelings. What attracts him in the poets we have just mentioned is precisely their art of transposing everything into symbolic pictures, of making multiple resonances vibrate under one word. Now M. Debussy's music does not seize upon the evocative meaning of these poems in the manner of ordinary music. His effort seems to be to note the most distant harmonics of the verse and to take possession of all the suggestions of the text in order to transport them to the realm of musical expression. Most of his compositions are thus symbols of symbols, but expressed in a language itself so rich, so persuasive, that it sometimes reaches the eloquence of a new word, carrying its own law within it, and often much more intelligible than that of the poems on which it comments. Such is the case, for example, with *L'Après-midi d'un faune.*

THE FAUN
(December, 1903)

* * * Never more than under the direction of M. Pierné have I enjoyed the incomparable charm exercised by the *Prélude à "L'Après-midi d'un faune"* of M. Debussy. This music, somehow imponderable, as if located at the outer edges of the world of intelligible harmonies, which remains nevertheless always and above all music, and even extremely clear and persuasive music, requires a performance at once utterly poetically free and meticulously exact. That of last Sunday was so supple and so clean that the character of a miraculous orchestral improvisation which it should have was fully evident: the piece, having become transparent to the most near-sighted eyes, was encored by cheers.

The strangest and rarest thing was that the second playing surpassed the first in warmth and precision.

ERNST DECSEY

[A Jewel Among Masterpieces]†

Ernst Decsey (1870–1941) was a leading critic in Vienna from 1908 to 1938. His four-volume biography of Hugo Wolf (Berlin, 1903–06) remains his greatest claim to wider fame, but his two books on Debussy deserve attention too.

* * * This afternoon, one might say, meant a Sunrise.

The short *Prelude*—only 110 measures—shows Debussy's inventive spirit in its themes, its construction, and its colorful instrumentation. A stream of beautiful music flows toward the listener from the first flute solo, and one forgets that this music means to illustrate something too. Managing with the usual classical orchestra (strings, woodwinds, four horns, no trombones, no trumpets, only English horn and two harps)

† Decsey, *Debussys Werke*, Graz, 1948, pp. 77–83. Translation by the editor.

the artist paints a scene of pagan sensuality.

With Mallarmé it is the faun—half man, half beast, with horns and hoofs—who sleeps on Etna in the sultry afternoon sunshine, and dreams lascivious dreams behind closed eyelids.

Obsessed by sweet fantasies, he sees the beautiful nymphs with an incarnadine glow. He thinks that he is about to grasp their beauty, but they vanish; all remains dreams. All this is easily conceived. And the plastic power of music makes it clearer than poetry, the beautiful bodies of the nymphs, lured by the syrinx, appear in the D♭ section with hallucinatory clarity.

But what is inconceivable is the formal principle observed by the artist, which places him, whether he followed it consciously or instinctively, among the greatest masters of form.

Prominent throughout the piece, from the first measure on, is the melodic interval of a fourth and the combined intervals, second and third. The first theme of the solo flute contains this as tritone (C♯-G). The great D♭ theme (p. 47 of the score) contains it (A♭-F-E♭). The coloraturas of the woodwinds (p. 40) and even the progression of the contrabasses (D♭-G, p. 47). The artist's will to unification penetrates everywhere, shaping everything. * * *

The introduction evokes an Arcadian mood in its few bars, partly through the sun-glinting harp glissando, partly through the blissful call of the horns, which sound like someone talking in his sleep, but above all through the tonal wreathing of the low flute, which in this register sounds penetrating, indeed hypnotic, as if it were the strongest instrument of the orchestra. And four times it repeats its call, each time with a different harmonic allure. But now, provisionally passing by the magic of the impression, we want to investigate in a sober way what Debussy, the "formless" musician, the vague impressionist, the composer of haziness, has constructed with this material.

The piece began with the exposition (4 measures), followed by a postlude derived from it (6 measures), altogether 10 measures.

At rehearsal number 1 begins the repetition of these first 10 measures, that is, a second follows the first *Stollen*.

Now at number 2 what follows these two *Stollen* is an *Abgesang* (with the theme surrounded by the sparkling harps), again 10 measures long.

This *Abgesang*—N.B.—consists of its own two *Stollen* and its own *Abgesang*. And the first *Stollen* (of the *Abgesang*) is 2 measures long, the second *Stollen* (of the *Abgesang*) is 3 measures long (up to the 12/8 measure), whereupon the *Abgesang* (of the *Abgesang*) begins, comprising 5 measures (up to number 3). Thus again 10 measures.

So far then, in the first 30 measures, the piece had the form of a *Bar* —two *Stollen* and an *Abgesang*, with the *Abgesang* itself shaped as a *Bar* as well—an intricate construction, which appears graphically approximately thus:

First Part
1st *Bar*

1st *Stollen*: 4 measures flute solo, 6 measures postlude, horns using for this motives from both measures of the theme.
2nd *Stollen*: the theme harmonized, again with postlude (horns, oboes) altogether 10 measures.
Abgesang (in *Bar* form)
    Abgesang: theme dissolves into thirty-second-note passage, 5 measures.
    1st *Stollen:* theme varied, with harp acc., 2 measures.
    2nd *Stollen:* theme varied, with harp acc., 3 measures.

(The entrance of a new *Stollen* is always recognized by the beginning of the same theme. Whereas poetry has its rhyme at the end, the rhyme of music always stands at the beginning.)

To this first articulated part (in *Bar* form) there now succeeds a second section, which consists of *two middle parts*.

The first of these middle parts begins at number 3 of the score, is 24 measures long, and extends to the entrance of the D♭ (p. 47 of the score). This first middle part is followed by a second middle part, likewise of 24 measures, that is, from the D♭ (p. 47) to p. 53, E major, number 8.

The *first middle section* is characterized by "echo" passages, wind coloraturas, that run along the whole-tone scale and overlap each other.

Its first *Stollen* embraces 3 measures, its second *Stollen* again 3. Its *Abgesang* begins at number 4 with the oboe and includes 7 measures up to number 5.

The *second middle section* brings on a splendid big song of the winds, one of Debussy's most beautiful melodic inspirations.

But even this singing middle section consists of two *Stollen* and an *Abgesang,* whose beginnings are quite clear (first *Stollen* 8 measures, second *Stollen* 8 measures, *Abgesang* 8 measures, all together 24 measures).

E major enters, the reprise follows, resuming the beginning and leading to the end. This too is a *Bar*, 31 measures long, while the *Bar* of the beginning counted only 30 measures (3 × 10): a demonstrable and also quite perceptible relation of equilibrium.

The whole *Afternoon of a Faun* accordingly consists of three parts:
    a first, expository section (30 measures)
    a second section (consisting of two middle parts, 48 measures)
    the third or recapitulatory section (31 measures)
and each of these parts and sections is in *Bar* form.

Enough of our sober tone. We have dissected the poor *Faun*'s body and investigated his skeleton, and though this musical-anatomical procedure may be unpoetic, something full of poetry comes to light. We discovered in Debussy the *Bar* form, the same principle of construction that A. Lorenz discovered in Richard Wagner. Now we ask: how does it happen that two such utterly different masters, the French and the German, the nondramatist and the dramatist, followed this principle? Obviously because the form of the *Bar*—AAB—seems to be a primordial form of human thought in general: two premises from which a conclusion is drawn. The same idea of construction, moreover, supports the sonnet. Hence one may sum up: the *Faun Prelude* has its inexplicably poetic effect because it is carried by the classic form of the sonnet, in its broadest outline.

So far everything has been rationally explained, the motivic development (the second-third progression) as well as the structural outline. From here on no more can be explained; all explaining seems to escape into symbols, metaphors, mere verbiage. No matter whether the first flute melody be felt as Oriental, Russian, Arabic, or Greek—the thought may occur to us that a musician may master all these refinements, that he may compose a great sonnet all from the nucleus of a fourth, and yet that he may fail in his music because his invention has nothing to communicate to our feeling. For with a master like Debussy, besides all the material and besides the forming instinct there is also precisely the enigmatic, inexplicable musical inspiration.

Four times the syrinx melody sounds at the beginning, four times it sounds at the end, as noted, each time harmonized differently and so surprisingly that we might think the key had been found each time uniquely. (Compare the last entries in E, in E♭, and then on C♯, pp. 56, 59, and 61.) The dreamy change of the harmony testifies not only to the master's joy in the elementary nature of sound, but also his playful sense of power over the material. As the poet governs the connections of words, so the musician does his chords, which approach, withdraw, transform themselves all according to his command. And since all this is presented as if by necessity, as if it had always been so, it bears the sign of mastery.

Just as admirably Debussy's rhythmic power grew. The entrance of the first middle section (number 3) is clearly set off by the eighth notes of the harp and the scratching of the cellos. Marvelous is the yearning, wavelike progress of this part, its impatience for the D♭ part. Then the D♭ song of the second middle part itself is one of the full-blown broad melodies, such as can be found only in a master's youth: it enchants by the gracefulness of its curve, which has the erotic effect of a beautiful woman's torso. Note further at number 10 the warm embracing of the body of the theme (muted violins and flutes) and the fading away with the entry of the antique cymbols, while two horns, sweetly blended with a violin, lead to a farewell tender as a breath. As in many piano pieces, as in *Fêtes* or *Sirènes*, here too Debussy is master of the fading away. One more melancholy glance back, and the ancient dream-world dissolves in the cymbals.

The *Prelude to "The Afternoon of a Faun,"* which owes its origin to a happy hour, is the jewel among Debussy's masterpieces.

PIERRE BOULEZ

[Modern Music Begins]†

Pierre Boulez (b. 1925) won international prominence among composers of his generation soon after World War II. His *Le Marteau sans maître* (1955) is widely regarded as one of the few classic achievements of its

† From Pierre Boulez, *Notes of an Apprenticeship*, trans. Herbert Weinstock, New York, 1968, pp. 344–45. Copyright © 1968 by Alfred A. Knopf, Inc.; reprinted by permission. Boulez's article was originally written for the Fasquelle *Encyclopédie de la musique*, Paris, 1958, I, 633. A recording of the *Faun* under Boulez's direction was issued in 1968 (Columbia MS 7361).

decade. His later compositions, his teaching, his occasional critical writings, and above all his conducting continued to spread his influence in the 1960s.

Undeniably, the *Prélude* gave proof of much greater audacity than the String Quartet; that doubtless was owing in large part to the poem, the extensions of which incited Debussy's thought to free itself of any scholastic impediment. This masterwork of Debussy's rapidly became the most popular of his concert works; it marked the decisive advent of a music merely foreseen by Mussorgsky. It has been said often: the flute of the *Faune* brought new breath to the art of music; what was overthrown was not so much the art of development as the very concept of form itself, here freed from the impersonal constraints of the schema, giving wings to a supple, mobile expressiveness, demanding a technique of perfect instantaneous adequacy. Its use of timbres seemed essentially new, of exceptional delicacy and assurance in touch; the use of certain instruments—flute, horn, and harp—showed the characteristic principles of the manner in which Debussy would employ them in later works. The writing for woodwinds and brasses, incomparably light-handed, performed a miracle of proportion, balance, and transparency. The potential of youth possessed by that score defies exhaustion and decrepitude; and just as modern poetry surely took root in certain of Baudelaire's poems, so one is justified in saying that modern music was awakened by *L'Après-midi d'un faune.*

JEAN BARRAQUÉ

[An Experiment Crowned with Success, 1962]†

Jean Barraqué (b. 1928) is the composer of piano music made famous by André Hodeir's book, *Since Debussy* (New York, 1961), and of a vast work in progress based on Hermann Broch's *Death of Virgil*. (See articles in *The Musical Times* by G. W. Hopkins, CVII [1966], 952, and Tim Souster, CX [1969], 66.) Barraqué is also the author of an important study, *Rythme et développement,* in *Polyphonie*, IX–X (1954), 47, containing analyses of works by Machaut, Stravinsky, Messiaen, and Boulez. His book on Debussy, though flawed by some mistakes that a full-time scholar would have avoided, is valuable for its fresh comments on the music.

With the *Prélude à "L'Après-midi d'un faune"* Debussy not only produced his first masterpiece, but undertook his first major experiment in the field of orchestration—an experiment crowned with the greatest success from the start. * * *

The profound novelty of the score lies in its poetic substance, but this results from an original formal conception. The form of the *Prélude à "L'Après-midi d'un faune"* is already typical of Debussy's thought: rejection of classical molds, of bithematic exposition, of rigorous development, for the sake of a sort of improvisation around a theme. Still the presence of developments, the juxtaposition of sections, and the different presentations of the opening theme make of the *Prélude à "L'Après-midi d'un faune"* a blend of traditional forms, a fusion of the achievements of sonata form (development), of the sectional construction of the song form (middle section), and of the procedure of variation. As in the song form, the middle section is independent of the two other wings, here symmetrical, surrounding it. The famous

---

† Barraqué, *Debussy*, Paris, 1962, pp. 85–90. Translation by the editor. Reprinted by permission of Editions du Seuil, Paris.

flute theme, always harmonized differently, is presented ten times. One can mark off six parts thus constituted:

1. Exposition of the principal theme and cadence on the dominant (up to number 3 of the score).
2. Development (from number 3 to the second measure of p. 47).
3. Middle section (up to number 8).
4. Development (up to number 10).
5. Recapitulation (up to number 12).
6. Coda.

It is easy to assert that the *Prélude à "L'Après-midi d'un faune"* belongs to the class of Lied form by virtue of parts 1, 3, 5; to sonata form by virtue of its development parts, 2 and 4, as well as by its fifth part which is related to a recapitulation by the presence of a second theme (this does not appear in an expository section, but in the first development).

I. This section comprises four expositions of the principal theme and a cadencing formula on the dominant of the principal key (E major). The principal theme, not harmonized, appears from the beginning with the flute solo. This marvelous theme presents curious correspondences associating certain melodic and rhythmic figurations. The first measures move within the limited space of the tritone. Corresponding with this almost irrational idea of the tritone Debussy uses a rhythmic irrationality in the descending motions (the triplet of sixteenths) but not in the ascending motions, which are associated with chromaticism. Although the accentuation remains classical, the use that Debussy makes of it is original. The preparation of the accent here is very long, and the accent itself—the B—is preceded by the widest melodic span: in two leaps the theme clears the interval of an octave. The second presentation of this theme in E major is harmonized, but in a lower key, in D major. The "real" harmonization—the one that gives an auditory satisfaction and an impression of sonorous fullness—occurs at the third exposition. The fourth exposition presents a rhythmic variant, which, however, has been announced in connection with the third exposition: rhythmic augmentation of the first note balanced by a diminution in the second measure of p. 39.

II. The development is in three parts. The first is a double presentation of the principal theme harmonized by chords of the whole-tone scale. The second part, where the second theme appears in the oboe (number 4), with its two elements, is a section of tonal motion in which the modulations prepare the lyrical expansion of the central part. The third part is a pedal on the dominant of D♭; it thus announces the key of the middle section.

III. The middle section in D♭, expressive paroxysm of the work, is composed of a big phrase in four periods and based on two elements: the first, very expressive; the second (8 measures after 7) appearing in the third period, seems to be derived from a fragment of the second theme. These two elements are combined in the fourth period.

IV. This development presents the theme in augmentation in its sixth harmonization (number 8) and then, in a new variation, with the seventh harmonization.

V. At the beginning of the recapitulation the principal theme, in the flutes, is combined with the second element of the theme of the middle section and repeated with a ninth harmonization which seems to belong to no well-defined key, in spite of the presence of catalogued chords.

VI. The last harmonization, which coincides with the coda, establishes the theme on a tonic pedal. This amazing and famous page of five measures, often cited as a model of orchestration, ranks undoubtedly among the most beautiful moments in all music; over the pedal of the contrabasses, the theme, first sketched by two muted horns and a few low violins (a combination that makes a sonority unheard of at the time) is followed by the elliptical flute solo:

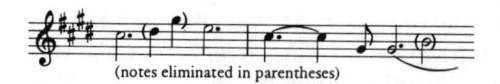

(notes eliminated in parentheses)

The theme has reached no destination. The crystalline sound of an antique cymbal, a few plucked notes of the basses. . . . A sort of fading of the sound into the distance seems to leave the work unfinished and the listener in suspense.

Some rather complex formal overlappings have nearly plunged the *Prelude* into confusion. But a profound unity of idiom saves the work from incoherence. The secret of this unity must be sought in the relation of a fundamental chord-progression, which assumes the whole structural weight of the score. To elucidate, this progression appears in the harmonization of the theme itself, as it is found in the course of the third exposition (harmonization in E). It is the presence of the tritone that produces this relation of the tonic to the Neapolitan sixth of the dominant (or lowered VI), or more generally a relation of a minor sixth.

Already in the second exposition in D we could doubtless have found the relation I-VI, with lowered fifth in the VI chord (but not the Neapolitan sixth of the dominant—number 1). But this progression had appeared even earlier in a rather mysterious way, and with a felicitious effect on the poetic level, in the first harmonic progression that the work presents (immediately after the exposition of the theme), followed by a measure of silence and then repeated.

In considering the relationship of the tonic notes suggested by these two chords (B and E♮) we discover the powerful link of the fundamental progression inverted (minor sixth inverted to major third). Such a discovery is not accidental; a meticulous analysis allows us to bring out of hiding, sometimes as if underground, the presence of this relation which is intrinsic in the theme itself. We might illustrate the pervasiveness of this true compositional material, consisting only—almost abstractly—of the idea of the sixth, by citing also the subtle relation of the progressions of keys: the middle section in D♮ should be regarded as enharmonically in C♯ major—the sixth of the principal key; the sixth and seventh harmonizations (E and C) at the beginning of the fourth part are in the relation of minor sixth. . . . Or again, in a more condensed form, the progressions of chords presented in the passage at the end of the work, with its two subdivisions (one measure after [number] 12).

Such concern for firmly assuring the unity of the work denotes a mind preoccupied with giving his works a formal balance. But Debussy wants this balance to be renewed and to be appropriate each time for each new work. The means that he is to use, moreover, are endlessly different. Thus the Debussy technique eludes any rule of procedure.

Bibliography

ON DEBUSSY AND HIS WORK IN GENERAL

Burk, John N., *Estimating Debussy*, in *New Music Review*, New York, XVIII (1919), 76.
    A judicious obituary article, placing Debussy in relation to French poetry and painting, and the international repercussions of all French influences.

Debussy, Claude, *M. Croche, the Dilettante Hater*, trans. with a foreword by L. Gilman, New York, 1928.
    Selected journal articles.

Frankenstein, Alfred, *Debussy: Orchestral and Vocal Works*, in *High Fidelity*, VIII/1 (Jan. 1958), 79.
    Excellent critical discography.

Goldsmith, Harris, and Conrad L. Osborne, *Debussy on Microgroove*, in *High Fidelity*, XII/9 (Sept. 1962), 66.
    More nearly up-to-date than the preceding entry. Six versions of the *Faun* are compared.

Keeton, A. E., *Debussy: His Science and His Music*, in *Nineteenth Century*, LXVI/391 (1909), 492.
    A remarkably penetrating though modest early evaluation.

Kremlev, Iulii, *Debussy*, Moscow, 1966.
    An excellent one-volume presentation (in Russian) of the life and works, incorporating the results of recent international scholarship, and including a good account of the *Faun*, pp. 255–70.

Lesure, François, *Bibliographie debussyste*, in *Revue de musicologie*, XLVIII (1962), 129.
    The most comprehensive published list of books and articles.

Lockspeiser, Edward, *Debussy: His Life and Mind*, 2 vols., London, 1962–65.
    The most thorough biography, with much fresh information.

Ottaway, D. Hugh, *Debussy as an "Old Master,"* in *Hallé Magazine*, XXXII (Jan. 1951), 13.

Vallas, Léon, *Claude Debussy: His Life and Works*, trans. by Maire and Grace O'Brien, London, 1933.

The revised French edition of 1958 should be consulted for some corrections of detail, but the translation is still valuable, especially for its thematic index.

——— *The Theories of Claude Debussy, Musicien Français,* trans. by M. O'Brien, Oxford, 1929 (reissued in paperback, New York, 1967).
Supplement to *M. Croche,* with emphasis on the patriotic side of Debussy's thought.

ON DEBUSSY IN RELATION TO MALLARMÉ

Fumet, Stanislaus, *Poème et mélodie: ou un mariage ingrat,* in *Revue musicale,* 210 (1952), 73.
Kesting, Marianne, *Mallarmé und die Musik,* in *Melos,* XXXV (1968), 45.
Lloyd, James Austin, *Mallarmé on Music and Letters,* in *Bulletin of the John Rylands Library* (Manchester, England), XLII (1959), 19.
——— *L'Après-midi d'un faune: essai d'explication,* in *Synthèses* (Brussels), 258/259 (1968), 24.
Lockspeiser, Edward, *Mallarmé and Music,* in *Musical Times,* CVIII (1966), 212.
Patri, Aimé, *Mallarmé et la musique du silence,* in *Revue musicale,* 210 (1952), 101.
Phillipps, C. Henry, *The Symbolists and Debussy,* in *Music and Letters,* XIII (1932), 298.
Schmidt-Garre, Helmut, *Rimbaud—Mallarmé—Debussy: Parallelen zwischen Dichtung und Musik,* in *Neue Zeitschrift für Musik,* CXXV (1964), 290.
——— *Mallarmé und der Wagnerisme,* in *Neue Zeitschrift für Musik,* CXXX (1969), 512-19.
Terenzio, Vincenzo, *Debussy e Mallarmé,* in *Rassegna Musicale,* XVII (1947), 132.
Wenk, Arthur, *Debussy and the Poets,* dissertation, Cornell University, 1970.

ON THE PRELUDE

Lockspeiser, Edward, *Debussy . . . facsimile,* in *Music and Letters,* XLV (1964), 301.
Mondino, Luis Pedro, *Prélude à l'après-midi d'un faune de Claudio Debussy: estudio completo de la obra y guia para la audición . . .* (Buenos Aires, 1946).
Mondino divides the piece into twenty parts; he discusses two recorded performances, and attempts to specify correspondences between particular sounds and particular details of the poem.
Munro, Thomas, *"The Afternoon of a Faun" and the Interrelation of the Arts,* in *Journal of Aesthetics and Art Criticism,* X (1951), 95; and in his *Toward Science in Aesthetics: Selected Essays,* New York, 1956, p. 342.